"I'r[illegible] Sorr[illegible]sh Culture 101

A Hilarious Guide to British Culture, From Fish 'N' Chips to Brexit, and Everything In between

Jeff Watson

Contents

Chapter 1

Test Your Knowledge With Our Free British Culture Quiz!

Think you've got what it takes to navigate the quirks and charms of British culture?

Simply scan the QR code below to dive into a series of fun and challenging questions that will put your understanding of British culture and slang to the test.

- Test your British knowledge in a fun and interactive way
- Challenge your friends and impress them with your results
- Deepen your understanding with questions tied directly to the book
- Learn and laugh as you uncover quirky British traditions

So grab a cuppa, scan the code, and let's find out just how British you really are!

SCAN ME

Bonus Audiobook Included!

Dive deeper into the quirks and charms of British culture on the go! With your Amazon purchase, enjoy a complimentary audiobook version of the entire book. Just scan the QR code below to access the Google Drive folder instantly. Perfect for listening anytime, anywhere—immerse yourself in British wit, etiquette, and humor, hassle-free!

SCAN ME

A Quick Disclaimer

This book is written for lighthearted reading, blending cultural insights with humour to offer an entertaining exploration of British culture. While we aim to inform, we also indulge in well-known stereotypes and playful exaggerations for comedic effect. The tone is steeped in irony and satire, echoing the spirit of British humour itself. So as you turn the pages, please keep in mind that our observations are designed to amuse as much as they are to enlighten. So sit back, enjoy the ride, and remember: sometimes it's best to drop the stiff upper lip and have a ol' good laugh!

And... A Cheeky Favour to Ask

Thank you for picking up this hilarious guide to British culture! We hope it fills you with laughs and a few "Aha!" moments about the quirky, delightful world of Britain. If you enjoy the journey, we'd be chuffed if you could take a moment to share your thoughts in an Amazon review. Your feedback means the world to us and helps others discover this little book of British charm. Thanks ever so much for your support—enjoy the adventure!

SCAN ME

Chapter 2

"I'm Terribly Sorry"

Mastering British Politeness: The Art of the Apology

> **"The readiness of the English to apologize for something they haven't done is remarkable."**
> — Henry Hitchings

"I'm terribly sorry, but will pink do for the maps?" the manager of the print works asked.

"Pink?!"

"Yes, I'm frightfully sorry, but the red we normally associate with the British Empire, the red of our soldiers' uniforms, is just too dark. You see, the country names won't stand out and nobody will know which part of the empire they're in."

So pink it was. When you look at an old map or globe, you can see giant pink swathes marking territories where the sun never set on the British Empire. But set it did; most notably when the Union Jack was lowered in Hong Kong on July 1st, 1997 and the island was handed back to China, marking the end of the British Empire's 156-year rule in one of its last strongholds in Asia.

This chapter isn't about the empire, though. We'll take you on in a brisk gallop through a thousand-plus years of British dominance, decline, and the curious reasons why Britain is considered "Great" in Chapter Ten. For now, let's get back to the subject at hand: the three most quintessentially British words you'll ever hear: "I'm terribly sorry".

Incessant apologising permeates every facet of daily life in Britain. You'll hear variations such as "I'm frightfully sorry", which is a bit old hat now, often replaced by the more contemporary "I'm so sorry," with emphasis on the 'so' to convey the gravity of your regret.

From the moment you set foot on British soil, you'll notice that everyone apologises profusely all the time. It's a compulsive habit we've cultivated to keep things civil in any situation. Practice makes perfect so start right away and you'll soon fit right in.

Sorry... (But It's Not My Fault!)

Picture yourself in a cafe. You order a coffee from the waitress and the exchange goes something like this:

"Sorry, but could I have a coffee, please?"

The waitress arrives with your coffee, perhaps with a bit more enthusiasm than you'd expected, spilling some of the coffee... What do you do?

Naturally, you apologise. "I'm sorry, but do you have a tissue?"

That's the proper response, even though you're the customer and should be the one receiving the apology. Complaining just isn't the British way. Instead, we mutter, mumble and quietly suffer in polite silence.

For a real-life demonstration, visit any supermarket (grocery store) and grab a trolley (cart). As you navigate the narrow aisles, you'll find there's hardly enough room for two trolleys to pass.

Naturally, you'll apologise, repeatedly, as will the other shoppers. It's a symphony of apologies, each one delivered in a tone so polite and subdued that you'll wonder if anyone really means it.

This brings us to...

The Orbit of Apologies

If you have to raise your voice to apologise to someone, it means that person is outside your 'apology orbit'.

Think of your apology orbit as a personal bubble extending only as far as your voice can carry. Inside this bubble your apologies are not only expected, they are required, and freely exchanged for even the most minor of infractions. Everyone within your apology orbit shares in the collective duty of maintaining civility through constant, low-key apologies.

But shouting "Sorry!" across a crowded room means you're venturing into someone else's apology orbit, where your apology might not be welcomed and it might even create confusion, for which, of course, you'll feel compelled to apologise.

That's why you'll hear a chorus of "sorrys" in supermarkets as shoppers manoeuvre their trolleys around the isles. Everyone is within their own orbits, and each "sorry" is a small acknowledgment of shared space and mutual inconvenience. It's a dance of politeness that keeps the peace in crowded situations.

The British apology is more than admitting fault (even when it's not your fault). The choice of words, tone and volume of an apology is an instrument that we've finely tuned over centuries for maintaining social harmony. It's a way of acknowledging that on a densely populated island, we're all bound to bump into each other, literally and figuratively. A quick "sorry" is usually the best way to smooth things over.

And don't worry if you ever find yourself outside of someone's apology orbit. Someone else will take care of it. After all, we're all in this together, and there's no need to make a fuss. Just say "sorry" and carry on.

Chapter 3

"Are You in the Queue?"

The Sacred Unspoken Rules Behind Britain's Queuing Etiquette

"Queuing is a time where British people can practice their hobby of tutting and sighing."
— Bill Bailey

If there's one thing that epitomises the spirit of British civility, it's the art of queuing. Standing in line is a sacred ritual of decorum that defines who we are. In a world of chaos and unpredictability, the queue is a beacon of order – a quiet affirmation that despite all the wrongs in the world fairness still exists.

Forming a queue of equally-spaced individuals, each respecting others' apology orbits, was especially important during the days of rationing during the world wars. With it came the necessity of waiting your turn, accepting your lot and getting on with it. Complaining was for the weak. What mattered was that everyone got their fair share, no matter how long it took, and no matter your social status. This wartime mentality seeped into the national consciousness, and today, it's as if queuing is encoded in the British DNA.

The sanctity of the queue is not to be trifled with. Woe betide anyone who breaks these unwritten rules. Nothing raises indignation levels higher or quicker than the filthiest of all humans...

The Queue Jumper

Absolutely no one is above the rules when it comes to queuing. There are no exceptions, even for celebrities and prime ministers, who are expected to join the end of a queue just like everyone else, whether waiting for a bus or lining up to pay respects to a deceased monarch.

For a society built on the values of patience and fairness, the queue jumper represents everything that's wrong with the world.

Picture the scene. You're standing in a queue that's been growing in length for several days as people line up for the latest iPhone to go on sale; the anticipation growing as you inch closer to the front. You're part of something larger; a collective experience of shared waiting, where everyone understands that their turn will come. Suddenly someone brazenly steps ahead, disregarding the sacred order. The outrage is immediate and palpable. A ripple of shock spreads through the queue, accompanied by sharp glances and mutters of disapproval. If the offence is severe enough, a pointed "Excuse me, there's a queue here!" wll ring out. The collective indignation unites everyone in silent solidarity against the queue jumper. It's a breach of the social contract that cannot go unpunished.

Ask most people on the streets today what the punishment should be for queue jumpers and they'll likely advocate for reviving the death penalty.

In fact the careers of 'This Morning' breakfast TV hosts Holly Willoughby and Phillip Schofield were unceremoniously killed off after public outrage at seeing the presenters use a back door to Westminster Hall when the late Queen Elizibeth was lying in state, while celebrities such as Elton John, Mick Jagger and David Beckham all waited patiently for hours to file past the queen's coffin with everyone else.

Fun Fact: About 250,000 mourners formed a 10-mile long queue to file past the late Queen Elizabeth II's coffin as she lay in state in Westminster Hall for six days in September 2022. However, her father, George VI, commanded a queue of 305,806 when he was lying in state in the hall in 1952.

The Queue Jumper

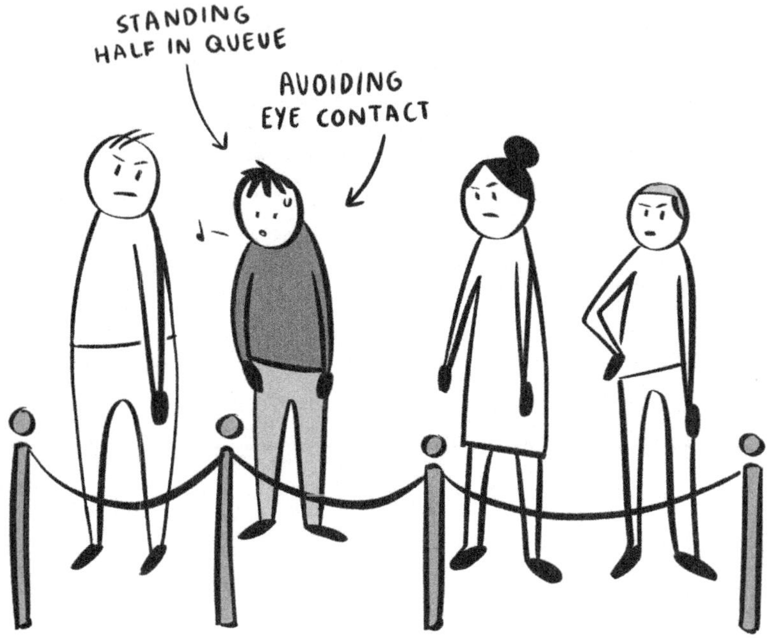

Admittedly, capital punishment for queue jumping might be a bit harsh. We are a forgiving bunch after all. Perhaps a more just punishment would be to put the perpetrator in a queue that never moves, placing them sufficiently far forward to think they'll soon be served. It would be a queue jumper's hell on earth to be perpetually waiting but never quite getting anywhere.

Now let's delve into...

The Unwritten Rules of Queuing

First and foremost: never, ever switch queues just because you think another line is moving faster. Doing so is the cardinal sin of queuing, and it's a mistake that even seasoned queuers have made at least once. The moment you abandon your queue for another, the one you left will inevitably surge forward, leaving you stranded and cursing your impatience. The same rule applies in all aspects of British life, from supermarkets to motorways.

When motorway queues morph into traffic jams, the British stiff upper lip is really put to the test as cars inch along at a snail's pace, halted completely by the dreaded signs warning of congestion ahead. Unlike standing in a queue, which can have its own peculiar charm, the motorway queue is a true test of endurance.

Drivers mutter angrily to themselves as they edge forward in a futile attempt to glimpse the cause of the holdup. Yet more often than not, after an hour of inching forward, the reason for the delay remains a complete mystery as traffic suddenly starts moving again.

Take a ride on the London Underground and you'll find the rules for queuing are strict and unyielding. After being reminded to "mind the gap", you'll find yourself at the mercy of the unspoken rule; that you must wait for everyone to exit the train before you board. Failing to observe this rule will result in a barrage of disapproving looks. The dark glares and tutting that follow are enough to make even the most hardened commuter think twice before rushing to grab a seat.

Every Queue is Sacred

At its core, queuing in Britain is more than just a practical necessity; it's a psychological balm. In a world that often feels unpredictable, the queue offers a structured pause where everyone knows their place. It's a quiet reminder that no matter how chaotic life gets, there's always a line to stand in. As long as you wait your turn, everything will work out in the end.

So as you navigate the post office, supermarket and motorway queues of Britain, remember that the queue is sacred. Respect it, honour it, and resist the urge to commit the ultimate sin of jumping ahead.

Chapter 4

"Wait, Are We in England?"

Decoding the Many Names for the UK

> **"When people say England, they sometimes mean Great Britain, sometimes the United Kingdom, sometimes the British Isles — but never England."**
> — George Mikes

Having landed and navigated the labyrinth of Heathrow or Gatwick airport, you hop into a taxi and the driver strikes up a conversation. "First time in the UK?", he asks. You nod, feeling a bit proud of yourself for knowing that "UK" stands for the United Kingdom. But then it hits you; what exactly does the United Kingdom mean? Is it the same as Great Britain, and where does England fit into all of this?

Your excitement is soon replaced by a nagging confusion. You thought you were in England, but now you're not so sure.

Let's break it down. The United Kingdom is made up of four countries: England, Scotland, Wales and Northern Ireland. So, when you're in London, you're in England, which is part of Great Britain, which in turn is part of the United Kingdom. Simple, right? Well, there's a bit more to it than that.

If you are actually in the 'City of London', the central business district of Greater London, you're in a square mile of land controlled by The City of London Corporation, which has its own government, mayor, police force and its own laws, flag and coat of arms.

Great Britain

Great Britain refers to the largest island that houses England, Scotland and Wales. But that doesn't include Northern Ireland, which is on the island of Ireland. The term 'Britain', on the other hand, is often used informally to refer to the entire UK, but that's not entirely accurate, either. Confused? Don't worry, you're not alone. Most Brits would struggle to give you a clear answer to your question.

The British Isles

The British Isles on the other hand is a geographical term that includes over 6,000 islands; the two largest of which being Great Britain and Ireland. The British Isles encompass both the UK and the Republic of Ireland, which is a completely separate country from the UK. So when someone mentions the British Isles, they're talking about the whole archipelago, not just the UK.

So why all the different names?

It all boils down to our chequered history over centuries of wars, treaties and political manoeuvring that's given us this complex patchwork of characteristics. Each term reflects a different aspect of the British identity, whether it's the political unity of the UK, the geographical reality of the British Isles or the cultural heritage of Great Britain.

Fun Fact: England is the largest country of the UK, covering 50,372 square miles and packed with a population of 56.5 million people. Scotland is the second largest (30,425 sq mi) and houses about 4.5 million people. Wales covers 8,024 sq mi and has a population of just over 3 million and Northern Ireland is 5,533 sq mi with a population of 1.9 million.

The Commonwealth and Crown Dependencies

But the confusion doesn't end there. When talking about things like the Commonwealth, Crown Dependencies and the British Overseas Territories, things get even murkier.

The Commonwealth is a political association of 56 member states, most of which were once part of the British Empire. The British Overseas Territories such as Bermuda and the Falkland Islands are remnants of the British Empire that remain under British sovereignty.

Crown Dependencies such as the Isle of Man and the Channel Islands are self-governing possessions of the British Crown but they aren't part of the UK. The Isle of Man in the Irish Sea has been self-governing since 979 AD, making it the oldest continuous parliament in the world.

Mann, as it's colloquially known by its inhabitants, the Manx – a hardy mix of Manx Gaelic-speaking Celts and Vikings – was ruled by the Scottish crown for a whisker shy of half a century, until the British crown acquired lordship in 1764. However, the island was never incorporated into the United Kingdom and so today the Manx enjoy a much higher standard of living than their subjugated British counterparts in a temperate tax haven dotted with casinos, yacht clubs and the occasional tailless Manx cat.

Every summer the Isle of Man's tranquillity is shattered by the roar of motorbike engines as adrenaline junkies let rip around the island's bendy mountain roads and zip through villages in the blink of an eye in the TT; the Isle of Man Tourist Trophy races.

The Channel Islands of Guernsey and Jersey bask in a little more sunshine than most rain-fatigued Brits on the mainland. The islands are closer to France than Britain, resulting in a mixed population of Norman, French and British descendants, along with native inhabitants, the Chumash, who were renowned makers of shell bead money.

The Channel Islanders have the best of both worlds. They self rule with their own laws, taxes and dominionship over purebred cows revered for producing the best butter in the world, while having British armed forces on their side. In fact the islands were the only part of the British Isles that German forces were briefly able to occupy during World War II, before being sent packing by the British army, keeping the islands' butter industry intact.

Pride and Prejudice

But what do you call the people living in these different parts of the British Isles? Are they British, English, Scottish, Welsh or Northern Irish?

It depends who you ask. Angus from Edinborough will proudly proclaim his Scottish ancestry as his nationality while Taffy from a town with a name you can't pronounce will insist he's a thoroughbred Welshman. Our brethren in Northern Ireland though are still a bit confused. They're either Irish or British, or both.

While the Welsh have invented words like 'popty-ping' to describe the modern microwave, the Irish and Scots with their shared Celtic heritage both have the ability to be profoundly poetic in their sarcasm and slang. They perform their best linguistic acrobatics in fits of rage, examples of which can be seen in What's the Craic? Irish Slang 101.

Another book in our hilarious series, and a must read to fully appreciate the charm of the Irish language and culture.

Despite our complex identities, regional pride is deeply ingrained in the eclectic British culture, which you'll encounter all over the country. While they're all part of the UK, they're fiercely proud of their individual cultures, languages and traditional butter making techniques.

Chapter 5

"God Save the Quee... Er, King"

The Royal Family: Scandals, Tradition and Protected Swans

> **"Of the various forms of government which have prevailed in the world, an hereditary monarchy seems to present the fairest scope for ridicule."**
> — Edward Gibbon

"Did you hear what Harry and Meghan just said on Oprah?"

"Honestly, I'm still trying to wrap my head around that Andrew interview. Can you believe the 'can't sweat' excuse?"

And so goes the conversation in pubs around Britain as locals sip their pints and mull over the latest royal news. Because in Britain, the royals aren't just a bunch of toffs in fancy hats. They're part of the national conversation, the subject of endless speculation, and honestly, more entertaining than the royal docudramas on the telly. Forget 'The Crown' on

Netflix. The real royal gossip is far juicier, and let's face it, much less predictable. Discussing the latest royal feuds is the ultimate distraction from the grey skies and soggy weather.

The Man Who Would Be King... Eventually

Let's start with the headline act: King Charles III. After an eternity waiting in the wings, Charles finally took his place centre stage in 2022 when he assumed the throne from his mother, the late Queen Elizabeth II. And what a glorious moment of good old British pomp and circumstance it was, pulled off with military precision after decades of planning and preparation.

Charles was always the more eccentric of the Queen's two sons, talking to plants and opining on everything from architecture to organic farming on the world stage.

Charles became king while the royals were embroiled in a quagmire of controversies, desperately trying to prove they were still relevant. But here's the thing; Charlie isn't just some quirky uncle who was suddenly put in charge. He's a man with a mission to drag the monarchy kicking and screaming into the 21st century. He's trimmed down the royal crew to a core team (sorry, not you, Andrew), and he's all about making the institution more streamlined, more efficient and hopefully more popular with a generation that's more likely to binge-watch 'Love Island' than tune in to the quee... Er, king's Christmas speech.

Let's face it, Charles had plenty of time to think about how to run things while he was waiting in the wings. His environmental activism – once dismissed as the ramblings of a green-thumbed prince – has aged like a fine organic wine. The once eccentric flower-whispering royal protégé now looks like he was way ahead of the curve. If only we'd listened sooner. Perhaps the planet wouldn't be having quite so many meltdowns (both the ice caps and royal tantrums...). But even with his eco-friendly creds, Charles has a tough job ahead. Modernising a thousand-year-old institution isn't exactly a leisurely walk in the royal gardens for a chat with the trees.

The Dodgy Duke of York

Charles's younger brother, Andrew, hasn't exactly helped elevate the royal family's status under the scrutiny of the British tabloids. The once dashing Duke of York's reputation took a nosedive quicker than you can say "Pizza Express in Woking" after his infamous 2019 Newsnight interview with Emily Maitlis, in which he tried to clear his name amidst the Jeffrey Epstein scandal. It was like watching a slow-motion car crash. And as for his excuse about not being able to sweat due to a medical condition, let's just say it left most of Britain raising an eyebrow and the rest of us frantically googling "do I have a sweating condition?".

Megxit - Coming to America

While the Duke of York's scandal cast a dark cloud over the monarchy, when the Duke and Duchess of Sussex (Prince Harry and Meghan Markle) departed the royal fold, the drama was a full-blown thunderstorm. The Sussexes' decision to step back from royal duties and head to sunny California was a royal mic drop. "Megxit", as it's now known, made Brexit look like a cosy afternoon tea. Harry and Meghan didn't just walk away; they sprinted, abandoning their Frogmore Estate cottage having just spent £2.4 million of taxpayers' money on renovations, leaving in their wake a whirlwind of tabloid speculation and family tension fuelled by more Oprah interviews than you could shake a stick at.

Harry and Meghan's move to America was a modern-day version of The Great Escape but instead of digging tunnels they packed up their royal titles and swapped windswept Windsor for the celebrity enclave of Montecito in Santa Barbara. And the bombshells didn't stop there. Allegations of racism, family rifts and struggles with mental health all came pouring out in their Oprah tell-all, and in the pages of Harry's autobiography, Spare, which indeed spared no details of his turbulent childhood and love life. Suddenly the Royal Family found themselves facing more scrutiny than someone committing the transgression of putting the milk first in their cup of tea.

Tradition Reigns Supreme

But here's the kicker. Despite all the scandals, the Royal Family remains as much a part of British culture as fish and chips and endless chats about the weather. You'll see their fingerprints everywhere as you journey through the country. Street signs, parks, statues... They're all reminders of the Royals' influence. But you'll also notice that Britain is changing and the Royal Family is scrabbling to keep up.

The Royals have always been about tradition, and boy, do we Brits love our traditions. There's the Changing of the Guard with their absurdly large bearskin hats and the Trooping the Colour, where the streets of London become a sea of red uniforms and Union Jacks. And who could forget the Queen's Christmas speech? Well, it was the Queen's Speech but now it's Charles's turn to continue the Yuletide tradition that was first televised in 1957, and we're all waiting to see if he'll sneak in a few words about composting between the festive greetings.

And let's not overlook the delightfully odd royal traditions that have survived through the centuries. Did you know for example that the King owns all the unmarked mute swans in Britain?

It's a Swan's Life

In an annual tradition dating back to the 12th century, the British Crown's "Swan Uppers" don red uniforms and row skiffs up the Thames in the third week of July to catch the swans so they can be weighed, measured and given a health check. It's part wildlife conservation, part historical pageantry, and distinctly British.

Then there's the Queen's bagpiper (now King's piper), who plays outside the monarch's window every morning. Because nothing says "good morning" quite like the ear-splitting shrill of a Scottish sheepskin being squeezed first thing in the morning, right?

But let's be real, tradition alone isn't enough to keep the Royals in the game. They've had to adapt – and fast. Younger generations aren't as enamoured with the idea of monarchy as their elders. For British youngsters, the notion of being born into a life of privilege simply because of your bloodline is, well, a bit outdated. The lavish lifestyles and the scandals, with the taxpayers footing the bill, is all up for debate in the country's pubs and social clubs.

But that's the great thing about Great Britain. Making fun of the monarchy is a national passtime, just as much for Zoomers (Gen-Z) as it was for the punk rockers of the 1970s. Even King Charles's trendy eco-friendly attitude didn't prevent him being targeted by environmental activists, who, in a comical display of vandalism, pasted cutouts of Wallace & Gromit cartoons on the first official portrait of the King. Anything goes it seems, in the land of free speech, until you kick a swan that is.

Fun Fact: Did you know that King Charles doesn't have a driving licence and never had to pass a driving test? Like his late mother, the monarch isn't required to have a licence or register their cars because driving licences are issued in the name of the monarch.

Is the End Nigh for The Windsors?

Well, the Royal Family is much more than a sideshow for the British public's entertainment. Whether we like it or not, our royal family is one of Britain's biggest exports. From state visits to Commonwealth tours, the Windsors are out there in front of flag-waving crowds, reminding the world that Britain still matters, and people are paying attention.

So what's next for the monarchy?

That's the million-pound question. Can King Charles and his streamlined crew keep the magic alive?

Will Prince William and Catherine manage to modernise the Royal Family without losing the traditions that make it uniquely British?

And what about Harry and Meghan, are they gone for good, or is there a chance they might pop back over the pond for a cameo?

One thing's for sure: the Royal Family isn't just going to fade into the background. They're too entrenched in the British psyche, too woven into the social fabric of this little island. And as long as there's a royal family, there'll always be enough drama to gossip about over a nice cuppa.

Chapter 6

"Mind The Gap!"

A Brisk Jaunt Through London and the Three Other Capitals of the UK

> **"When a man is tired of London, he is tired of life; for there is in London all that life can afford."**
> — Samuel Johnson

As your train pulls into a bustling London station, a calm yet commanding voice over the tannoy echoes "Mind the gap"; a phrase that's as iconic as Big Ben and the red double-decker buses snaking through the city's narrow streets. But "Mind the Gap" isn't just a practical warning about the space between the train and the platform. It's a metaphor for navigating the cultural and historical gaps that define and divide London, and indeed, the entire United Kingdom.

The Roman Outpost That Became the Beating Heart of the UK

London is more than just the capital of England. It's the city where centuries of history collide with the relentless pace of modern life. From the imposing grandeur of Buckingham Palace to the edgy street art of Shoreditch, London is a city of contrasting layers, where old and new coexist in a sometimes chaotic, always fascinating collage.

Before the red buses and black cabs there was Londinium, a Roman outpost established in AD 50, encircled by a wall containing the square mile that is the financial heart of the UK today.

London Bridge is situated in the same spot as the first bridge across the River Thames, which was built by the Romans. The Roman bridge is long gone but parts of the original London Wall remain to this day, tucked away between modern skyscrapers, a silent reminder that London's roots run deep, as we'll find out in the next chapter.

You'd be forgiven for calling the iconic clock tower of London's skyline Big Ben, which is actually the name of the 13-ton bell behind the clock face. The tower itself, unimaginatively known simply as 'The Clock Tower', was renamed Elizabeth Tower to celebrate the Queen's Diamond Jubilee in 2012. Standing tall over the Thames since the reign of Queen Victoria, the tower is symbolic of British stoicism and has borne witness to countless historic events, surviving the Blitz of World War II to ringing in a new millennium.

As you navigate the winding streets, you'll find that each London neighbourhood has its own distinct flavour. Westminster is the seat of the power and tradition of British governance with the Houses of Parliament and Westminster

Abbey standing testament to the city's political and religious history. Head east to the City of London and you'll find yourself in the financial heart of the UK, where glass skyscrapers tower over the remains of the Roman wall. Cross the river to the South Bank, and you're in a hub of culture and creativity, where the Tate Modern and Shakespeare's Globe Theatre sit side by side.

London is much more than a crusty remnant reserved for boring history books. The city is constantly reinventing itself. To experience the real London, hop on a red bus and head away from the tourist hotspots to areas like the East End, where you can still hear the echoes of Cockney rhyming slang of the suburbs, which were once the hunting grounds of England's most notorious twins, Ronnie and Reggie Kray, whose murderous reign of armed robbery, organised crime and 'Chelsea smiles' in the 1950s and 60s makes the Scicillian mafia seem like saints. Today the East End has a classier bohemian vibe but the likelihood of being robbed remains a very real threat when a cup of coffee costs an arm and a leg.

Edinburgh: The Seat of Scottish Enlightenment

If London is a city of contrasts, the capital of Scotland is a city of layers. Built on seven hills, with its ancient castle perched dramatically on a volcanic rock, Edinburgh's history is as rich as its whiskey. The Old Town with its medieval streets and narrow closes is a UNESCO World Heritage site while the elegant Georgian architecture of the New Town reflects the golden age of Edinburgh's role in the Scottish Enlightenment of the 18th century, during which art, music and architecture flourished.

Edinburgh Castle dominates the skyline as one of the oldest fortified places in Europe, serving as a royal residence, a military stronghold and even a prison since it was first built during the reign of Malcolm III in the 11th century. It's said the castle is haunted by the ghosts of prisoners kept there during the Wars of Scottish Independence; and the clank of their chains can be heard by those brave enough to tour the castle's dungeons.

In August, the entire city transforms into the world's largest arts festival, the Edinburgh Fringe. Performers, comedians, actors and acrobats descend on the city in their thousands, filling theatres and every street corner, where a Viking juggling flaming swords while reciting Shakespeare doesn't look at all out of place. It's just another layer of eclectic Edinburgh.

Edinburgh is also home to Arthur's Seat, an extinct volcano, atop which are the best views of the city. Legend has it that King Arthur and his knights held court here but you'll have to climb 822 feet to the summit to see for yourself if there's any truth to the tale. Just don't expect to find a round table at the top.

> **Fun Fact:** Edinburgh's Royal Mile, the historic road that runs through the heart of the Old Town, is actually a Scots mile, which is equivalent to about 1.2 English miles. So when you're walking down the Royal Mile, you're technically covering more ground than if you were south of the border... It's just another way the Scots do things a little differently.

Cardiff: Coalpits, Culture and Rugby

From Edinburgh, we travel west to Cardiff, the capital of Wales. Cardiff is the youngest of the UK's capital cities but no less rich in history and culture. Once a bustling coal port, Cardiff has reinvented itself as a vibrant, cosmopolitan city.

The revitalised Cardiff Bay area is now home to the iconic Wales Millennium Centre, a striking piece of architecture that's become a symbol of Welsh culture and creativity.

Cardiff historically powered the British Empire with its coal industry. The city's docks were the largest coal-exporting port in the world, and Cardiff's wealth was built on the black gold that flowed through its veins. Today the coal ships are gone but the city's industrial past is still evident in the architecture and the people who live there.

The city is anchored by Cardiff Castle, a fortress with a 2,000-year history. From its Roman foundations to its Victorian Gothic interiors, the Castle is a microcosm of the city's layered history. Visit during the summer and you could catch a medieval jousting tournament (more on that in Chapter 11), because who doesn't love knights in shining armour knocking each other off horses?

Cardiff is also home to Cardiff Arms Park, a shrine to the sport of rugby, which the Welsh adopted from the English as a national sport in 1850. On match days the city comes alive with a sea of red jerseys and the sound of passionate singing as fans belt out "Hen Wlad Fy Nhadau" (Land of My Fathers). It's an experience beyond sport. It's a celebration of Welsh identity.

The Welsh language is another offshoot of Gaelic and is still very much alive today. While you'll get by just fine speaking English in Wales, asking for directions is particularly challenging, when you're looking for villages with names such as Llanfairpwllgwyngyllgogerychwyrndrobwllllantysiliogogogoch – the Welsh town with the longest name.

Belfast: From Troubles to Triumph

Across the Irish Sea lies Belfast, the capital of Northern Ireland, which has undergone a remarkable transformation in recent decades after emerging from a 30-year guerrilla-nationalist conflict. "The Troubles" was a period of intense dispute between Unionists and Republicans from the late 1960s until the Good Friday Agreement in 1998. The Protestant unionists (loyalists) wanted Northern Ireland to remain part of the UK while the nationalists (republicans), who were predominantly Catholic, sought to unite with the Republic of Ireland. Since the Good Friday peace agreement ending The Troubles, Belfast has become a vibrant, welcoming capital with a thriving arts scene and a renewed sense of hope.

Belfast once played a significant role in the UK's industrial revolution as a ship-building hub. It was here that the RMS Titanic was built – a ship more famous for its tragic end than the engineering marvel it was for its time. The story of the ill-fated ocean liner, from conception to its doomed voyage, is retold by those who built it at the Titanic Belfast museum, a striking piece of star-shaped architecture said to resemble the logo of White Star Line. Honestly though, it looks a lot like a massive iceberg; irony that didn't escape the judges of the Carbuncle Cup, an award given for the ugliest new building in the UK.

The Cathedral Quarter on the other hand, with its cobblestone streets and buzzing bars, is doing a better job at making Belfast a contemporary cultural hub. Here you can find everything from traditional Irish music sessions to cutting-edge art galleries. And if you're a fan of street art, you'll love the murals that decorate the walls, each one telling a story about the city's complex history.

Belfast is also the birthplace of legendary footballer George Best, one of the world's first soccer superstars. Known for his incredible talent on the pitch and his equally legendary exploits off it, Best remains a beloved figure in Belfast, so much so that they've even named the airport in his honour.

The Great British Melting Pot

As we wrap up this whirlwind tour of the UK's capitals, let's take a moment to appreciate just how much we've packed into this journey. London, with its mix of royal pomp and gritty street art, shows us that tradition and rebellion can not only coexist but thrive. Edinburgh, perched on its ancient volcanic rock, proves that history isn't just something you read about; it's something you feel, especially when wearing a kilt.

Cardiff, the underdog turned cultural heavyweight, reminds us that even the youngest cities can carry the weight of history with grace. And then there's Belfast, a city that has shed its troubled past, and now strides confidently into the future with the swagger of George Best on a victory lap.

More than just destinations on map, these cities are like four eccentric siblings at a family reunion, each with its own personality, its own quirks, and its own way of saying "You haven't really seen the UK until you've wandered my streets".

So as you head off on your next adventure, don't just mind the gap, leap into it. These cities are where the UK's essence collides with the present, creating a glorious blend of cultures, histories, and let's be honest, a bit of chaos. But that's what makes them so unmistakably British.

Chapter 7

"Two Thousand Years in Ten Minutes"

A Brief History of Britain: The Essentials

> **"The maxim of the British people is 'Business as usual.'"**
> — Winston Churchill

How does a tiny rain-soaked island in the North Atlantic become one of the most influential nations in history?

Britain's story is one of fierce battles, legendary monarchs and a stubborn refusal to be anything but extraordinary. From ancient warriors painted blue to the global empire that once ruled a quarter of the world, Britain's history is as colourful as it is complex.

The Birth of a Nation Ruled by Celts and Romans

Britain hasn't always been the sophisticated land of tweed and tea. It was once a wild and chaotic place inhabited by a hardy bunch of kilt-wearing tribes who painted themselves blue and charged into battle without a stitch of underwear. That's right, the word "Britons" is thought to come from a Celtic term meaning "painted people". These ancient warriors may not have had much fashion sense but they sure knew how to make a first impression.

Then the Romans arrived in 43 AD, bringing with them straight roads, heated baths and a love for order. They founded Londinium (modern-day London) and surrounded the city with a wall to keep out the locals, who weren't exactly thrilled with the Roman occupation. The Romans left their mark on everything from architecture to the English language, influencing the way we speak, live, travel and even keep track of days of the year.

Fun Fact: The Roman baths in the city of Bath are still standing as one of the best-preserved ancient Roman spas in the world. You can visit but bathing hasn't been allowed since 1978 following the death of a visitor infected by the deadly pathogen Naegleria fowleri after taking a dip in the geothermal spring water.

England Emerges from the Middle Ages

When the Romans packed up and left in the early 5th century (apparently they had more pressing matters back home), Britain was up for grabs. Enter the Angles, Saxons, and Jutes; tribes from what is now Germany and Denmark. They didn't exactly knock on the door; they barged in, swords drawn, and started carving out kingdoms. This era gave us the foundation of modern England, or 'Angle-land', as it was originally called.

Would peace reign for a while? Not a chance. The Vikings soon sailed in and things got a whole lot messier. These weren't your run-of-the-mill pirates though. They were expert sailors and ferocious warriors who left their mark on Britain in more ways than one. The Anglo-Saxon kings fought back, including the legendary Alfred the Great, and eventually a unified English nation began to take shape. It's thanks to this period that we have the foundations of English law, language, and, dare I say it, the love of a good underdog story.

> **Fun Fact:** We get the word "berserk" from the Vikings. The Norse warriors, known as the 'berserkers', fought with a frenzied rage that made them nearly unstoppable. Today, we might say someone has gone 'berserk; over a bad football call.

Power Plays and Pageantry

Fast forward to 1066, a year every British schoolchild knows by heart, to when William the Conqueror, the Duke of Normandy, sailed across the English Channel and took the English crown by force at the Battle of Hastings. With him came a new language (Old Norman French), new customs, and the infamous Domesday Book; a survey of England's lands and resources that's still used by historians today. William's reign marked the beginning of the Norman influence on Britain, which can still be seen in the country's legal system, language, and, of course, in the grand castles dotting the landscape.

But Britain wasn't done with drama. By the time we hit the 13th century, King John was forced to sign the Magna Carta in 1215, laying the groundwork for constitutional government. While the Magna Carta didn't exactly limit the king's powers overnight, it did spark the practice of holding authority to account – a tradition that's evolved into the modern-day British legal system

Fun Fact: The Magna Carta, though originally a peace treaty, is often celebrated as a cornerstone of democracy. A copy of the document is on display at the British Library in London, alongside works by Shakespeare and the original lyrics to the song Yesterday by The Beatles – another nod to Britain's cultural exports.

Tudor Drama and Defeating the Spanish Armada

By the 16th century, Britain was ready for a bit of a makeover. Enter the Tudors; a dynasty that turned England into a European powerhouse. Henry VIII, the king who had two of his six wives executed, founded his own church to kick off the English Reformation and separate the Church of England from the Catholic Church. This set the stage for centuries of religious conflict but also helped shape our British identity.

King Henry's daughter, Elizabeth I, continued the drama, defeating the Spanish Armada to pave the way for Britain's global empire. It was the era of exploration, piracy (privateering, as the English liked to call it), and the beginnings of Britain's growing influence around the world.

Fun Fact: Henry VIII's split from the Catholic Church was partly due to the pope refusing to let the king divorce his first wife, Catherine of Aragon, because her nephew was Charles V, the Holy Roman Emperor, who had just taken control of Rome. Today, Henry VIII is often remembered as the king who 'loved and left' six wives and left a complex legacy.

Charles II Restores Order Out of Chaos

The ensuing 17th century was quite chaotic. The English Civil War erupted between Royalists supporting King Charles I and Parliamentarians led by Oliver Cromwell. The war ended with the shocking execution of Charles I in 1649, briefly turning Britain into a republic. But the British love their traditions, and the monarchy was restored in 1660, when Charles II took the throne. Many 'great' events happened in the following decade. The Great Plague of London had already killed off about a quarter of London's inhabitants by the time the city was razed to the ground in the Great Fire of London in 1666. The fire nearly wiped out the walled city, destroying St Paul's Cathedral in the process. But the great fire marked the end of the great plague, and with it the rebirth of London as a modern metropolis with Christopher Wren commissioned to rebuild St. Paul's Cathedral in the trendy new baroque style of the roaring sixteen sixties.

This was also the era of coffeehouses, where men (and it was mostly men) gathered to discuss politics, science, and, occasionally, scandal. These coffeehouses are the ancestors of today's pubs, which we'll explore in the next chapter – a cornerstone of British culture if ever there was one.

Fun Fact: The Great Fire of London destroyed 87 churches, 13,200 houses, and St. Paul's Cathedral. On the bright side, it helped kill off the rats and fleas blamed for the bubonic plague, which eventually killed about 100,000 Londoners.

Full Steam Ahead for the Industrial Revolution

By the 18th and 19th centuries, Britain had transformed from a land of green fields and country estates into the 'Workshop of the World'. The Industrial Revolution brought about massive changes as factories, steam engines and railways spread across the country. It was an age of invention, when everything seemed possible, cementing Britain's reputation on the world stage as a hub of capitalist innovation.

Queen Victoria's reign saw the British Empire hit its peak with a reach that extended across a quarter of the world's maps. But it wasn't all tea and cucumber sandwiches in the homeland just yet. The Victorian era was also marked by stark social contrasts of immense wealth and dire poverty existing side by side; a reality captured in exquisite descriptive detail in the novels of Charles Dickens, whose works are an especially poignant read when you're stuck indoors on one of those typically rainy British days.

Fun Fact: It was said during the Victorian era that 'the sun never sets on the British Empire', which governed more than 400 million people across almost 14 million square miles of the planet. Today the empire is gone but far from forgotten. Its influence remains in the English language, the legal systems, and even the tea-drinking habits of many former colonies.

German Blitz Tests Britain's Resilience

The 20th century brought challenges that would test British resolve like never before. The First World War had left deep, unhealed scars and the Second World War brought the country to the brink of destruction. London was heavily damaged in the German bombing campaign, The Blitz, which lasted eight months and killed more than 40,000 civilians but Britain's spirit never wavered. Winston Churchill's famous 'Keep Calm and Carry On' attitude became a symbolic mantra of British resilience; a trait that remains deeply ingrained in the national character.

As Britain's empire began to dissolve following the world wars the country had to reinvent itself yet again. The post-war years brought the rise of the welfare state, the National Health Service (NHS), and a cultural explosion in the 1960s with the 'British Invasion' of music and fashion.

Fun Fact: The phrase "Keep Calm and Carry On" was originally a government slogan intended to boost morale during WWII. It was never widely used during the war but became a cultural icon in the 21st century, appearing on everything from mugs to T-shirts and tea towels.

Wrapping up Two Thousand Years

And there you have it, two thousand years of British history distilled into a few pages. Didn't think I could do it, did ya?

From painted warriors and Roman legions to Viking raids, Tudor intrigue and Victorian industry, Britain's story is one of constant change, adaptation and resilience. It's a tale of a small island that once ruled a global empire and today continues to play a leading role on the world stage.

So as you sip your next cup of tea or find yourself in a conversation about the weather, remember that you're part of a gripping story that stretches back millennia – of battles, beheadings, breakthroughs, and quirkiness. Whether you're here for the history, the culture or just the fish and chips, there's always more to discover in this endlessly fascinating Angle-land.

Chapter 8

"Two Pints of Lager, Please"

A Guide to British Pub Culture

"On Saturday afternoons in pubs around England, it seems as if the whole country has turned into a place of relaxation, laughter, and warmth."
— George Orwell

An Englishman, an Irishman and an Scotsman walk into a bar.

The pub door swings open and you're greeted by that unmistakable buzz – a mix of laughter, the clinking of glasses, and the low hum of conversation – that feels like home, even if you've never set foot here before. The air is thick with the scent of malt and hops, and somewhere in the background, the faint strains of a pub classic play on the jukebox.

If you really want to understand Britishness, start in a pub, a cornerstone of community life; a sanctuary where people from all walks of life come together to share stories, celebrate victories, and commiserate over losses. A British pub (a boozer) is a place where the boundaries of class blur, and where everyone, at least for a few hours, is part of the same tribe.

But what makes a British pub so special and revered in the hearts of the British people?

Well, pull up a stool, grab a pint and let's stumble through the essence of British pub life.

The Pub Crowd

Over there on your left you've got the usual suspects; a group of mates laughing louder than a football crowd. In the corner, a couple doing their best impression of a romantic drama, and at the far end the classic pub fixture: the lone regular. He's nursing his pint as if it's the last one on Earth, lost in thought, or maybe just trying to remember where he left his keys. In another corner stands a man quietly feeding coins into a fruit machine.

We're in a proper local, the kind of place where everyone knows your name, or will do after a few visits. It's got the lot: wooden beams that have seen more history than the Tower of London, a crackling fire that's more for atmosphere than heat, and a barmaid who's been here longer than the furniture. She gives you a nod as we head to the bar. You're in good hands.

The Art of Ordering a Pint

First things first. Let's get some pints on the go. Now don't just stand there like a tourist at rush hour. This is where you need to show some confidence. You'll want to order a pint, of course, because anything less would be, well, highly un-British. Whether it's a classic bitter, a smooth lager, or something a bit more adventurous like a craft ale, make sure you know what you want before you approach the bar. Nothing says "I'm new here" like dithering over the taps.

Once you've made your choice, lean in slightly, catch the barmaid's eye and give your order in a clear, confident voice. "Pint of lager, please". It's as simple as that. No need to mention the size. A pint is the default setting, just like the British weather is set to drizzle.

Oi, where's mine? Cheeky git...

When you're down the pub with yer mates, you buy drinks by the round. When it's your turn, you don't just buy for yourself; you buy for everyone in your group. It's a time-honoured tradition, and there's a certain art to it. Drinks are offered with the unspoken understanding that when the glasses are nearly empty, the offer will be reciprocated. So if you're up out of your seat, don't hesitate. Offer to get the drinks in, and make sure to ask what everyone's having. It's a smooth way to score social points and a great way to break the ice.

Don't worry. Your generosity will come back around when it's someone else's turn to get a round in. Just be prepared when the bill for that last round comes in. If you're in a bog standard Wetherspoons pub, you might get off lightly but some pubs will put a real dent in your wallet. But hey, it's all part of the experience, right?

In fact the etiquette of buying rounds is why we revere the pub so much. The gesture embodies the British sense of trust and fair play that's at the heart of community spirit. These previously unwritten rules of buying rounds were enshrined as Greaves' Rules, compiled by London journalist William Greaves, who drew on his many years experience of pubs and rounds. The Greaves' Rules were first published in the defunct Today newspaper as a Saturday morning essay and now internationally represent the spirit of drinking in an English pub.

Timeless Pub Culture

So you see, the local British pub is more than a drinking hole. It's a social hub, a gathering place where friends and strangers alike come together. The word 'pub' is short for 'public house', and that's exactly what it is – a house that's open to the public. Public houses have been part of British culture for centuries, some dating back to the 11th century. They've seen kings and queens come and go, wars start and end, and countless generations pass through their doors.

In many villages and towns, the local pub is the heart of the community. It's where people go to catch up on local gossip, celebrate birthdays, or even hold impromptu meetings. The pub is the great equaliser. Whether you're a CEO or a farmer, everyone's welcome, and everyone's on the same level once they've got a pint in hand.

Fun Fact: The oldest pub in Britain is claimed by several establishments, but one of the strongest contenders is Ye Olde Trip to Jerusalem in Nottingham, which dates back to 1189 AD. It's built into the caves beneath Nottingham Castle and was supposedly a stopping point for crusaders on their way to the Holy Land.

"Testing, testing... Is this thing on?"

Suddenly a high-pitched screech of feedback pierces the cosy hum of conversation, causing everyone to wince and a few pints to nearly spill. Big Dave, tonight's quizmaster, fumbles with the microphone, trying to find that elusive sweet spot between too loud and not loud enough.

"Alright, alright, settle down!", he finally bellows, swaying slightly as he clutches the microphone, his voice booming over the speakers. You can tell by his slurred words that he's had a few pints too many, but he's soldiering on with the kind of confidence only a true quizmaster can muster. "It's quiz night, and you know what that means... Get your drink... Er thinking caps on, and your pens ready!"

The pub quiz, a trivia contest usually held on a weeknight, is one of the most beloved pub traditions. Teams of friends (and sometimes strangers) compete to answer questions on a variety of topics ranging from general knowledge to obscure trivia. The prize might be anything from a round of drinks to a small cash prize. The real reward though is the bragging rights of having encyclopaedic knowledge.

Talking of quizzes, have you taken our free British Culture Quiz yet? Maybe you're curious to find out just how much you really know about the British... Jump to page X to find out!

As the night wears on the crowd changes. First the after-work crew heads home and is replaced by the evening regulars. Eventually the late-night crowd stumbles in, looking to stretch the night out as long as possible, before...

Ding ding ding!

The bell rings out, cutting through the chatter like a knife through butter. The landlord, a burly fellow with a face as red as the pub's carpet, leans over the bar with a grin.

"Last orders!" he calls, his voice carrying just the right mix of authority and cheer. You feel the collective pause in the room as everyone realises it's now or never for that final pint.

"Go on, then", you hear someone say at the next table, nudging their mate toward the bar. The bartender is already busy pulling pints with the efficiency of a well-oiled machine, the tap handles clinking as they're worked in quick succession.

As the clock hands edge nearer to closing time, the hum of conversation dips and glasses clink together one last time.

Friends exchange final toasts and the pub begins to take on that cosy, winding-down vibe that's so distinctly British.

And then it comes – "Time, ladies and gents!", the landlord's voice booms out again, this time with a hint of finality. You see regulars draining the last of their drinks, gathering up their coats and shuffling to the door. There's no rush though. The mood is relaxed, as if everyone knows they'll be back soon enough.

But you're not quite ready to leave yet. You take another sip, leaning back in your chair to soak it all in. This is the moment when the pub feels like a second home; a place where stories have been shared, laughs have been had, and where you've become part of the community.

As the last few stragglers head out, you finally stand, giving a nod to the bartender who's already wiping down the bar with the practised ease of someone who's done it a thousand times. "Cheers, mate", you say, and he gives you a smile that says, See you next time.

You'll be back soon enough.

Chapter 9

"Sort It Out, Ref!"

Divided and United by a Love of Sport

> **"Rugby is a good occasion for keeping thirty bullies far from the center of the city."**
> — Oscar Wilde

Shouts of joy, groans of despair, fists pounding tables... No, it's not a bar fight, but it might as well be. This is the sound of sport in Britain, where the stakes are always high, the emotions are always raw, and the outcome of a match can make or break your week. Whether it's football, cricket, rugby, or even a spot of tennis at Wimbledon, the Brits don't just watch sport, they live it.

In this chapter we're not just talking about scores or stats; we're diving into the very soul of British sport, where every match is a battle, every player a hero or a villain, and every fan a part of something much larger than themselves. So put on your lucky socks, grab a pint, and let's explore the rituals, the rivalries, and the sheer, unfiltered passion that make sport in Britain an experience like no other.

Football: It's Coming Home

Let's kick things off with the sport that turns even the most mild-mannered Brit into a roaring, face-painted fanatic. Football is followed in Britain like a religion, worshipped every Saturday as fans flock to stadiums, pubs, or their living rooms to watch their team battle it out on the pitch. The superstars of the Premier League and their multi million-pound deals might grab international headlines but the soul of British football lies in its grass roots of local teams, local rivalries, and an unrivalled level of passion.

Local derbies such as the North London Derby between Arsenal and Tottenham Hotspur or the legendary Old Firm clashes between Celtic and Rangers in Scotland are historical cultural events fueled by local pride. These rivalries go beyond the game, embodying the community identities and fierce loyalties that football nurtures across Britain.

Let's take a trip back to that unforgettable summer of 1966, a year etched indelibly in the nation's collective memory, as England hosts the FIFA World Cup. The nation is gripped with football fever and Wembley Stadium is a cauldron of noise. As the final whistle blows, England emerges victorious, winning the World Cup for the first time ever. Striker Geoff Hurst, one of the most prolific goal scorers ever, seals his place in history with the first and only (so far) hat-trick in the World Cup. His third goal was a controversial one with fans arguing whether the ball actually crossed the line.

Penalties seem to be England's Achilles Heel, though. We haven't won another World Cup trophy in more than 50 years. And when we did reach the quarter-finals against France in Qatar in December 2022, England missed a golden opportunity to equalise when Marcus Rashford hit a free kick over the goal in the 100th minute, giving France a 2-1 win.

But in a testament to great British sportsmanship, England was named winner of the FIFA Fair Play Trophy.

The fans are jubilant as Queen Elizabeth presents the trophy to captain Bobby Moore, cementing the moment as one of the most iconic wins in British sporting history. Geoff Hurst earned a knighthood for his hattrick and the victory song 'Three Lions (Football's Coming Home)' would later encapsulate the nation's enduring hope and love for the game.

Fast forward to 1999 and we find ourselves in Barcelona for the UEFA Champions League final. As the game enters injury time, Manchester United is trailing 1-0 to Bayern Munich but in a twist that could only be scripted in the most dramatic of films, United scores twice in quick succession. The fans go berserk. Man United's manager, Alex Ferguson, grins like a Cheshire cat and the phrase "Fergie time" is born. He became a Sir, too. It's moments like these that make football an all-consuming passion among the Brits.

Among the other global icons who have proudly donned the England shirt are David Beckham, with his legendary free-kicks and Hollywood flair, and more recently the likes of Harry Kane, Raheem Sterling, and Marcus Rashford. These players transcend the sport; becoming cultural icons and influencing everything from fashion to social justice. Rashford's campaign for free school meals during the COVID-19 pandemic, for example, earned him admiration far beyond the football world, proving that today's footballers can be heroes both on and off the field.

These modern stars continue to inspire, using their platforms for social good. Rashford's advocacy for children's welfare, Sterling's fight against racism, and Kane's leadership on and off the pitch demonstrate how football remains a powerful force for change, embodying the spirit of the sport as more than just a game but a driver of positive change in society.

Football's grip on the British psyche runs deep, going all the way back to World War I, when soldiers from opposing sides famously downed their weapons on Christmas Day 1914 to play a match in No Man's Land. It was a brief moment of humanity in the midst of unimaginable horror – a testament to the power of football to unite, even in the darkest times.

Today, football remains a living, breathing part of daily life. Whether it's the thrill of watching a last-minute winner or the agony of a penalty shootout loss, football evokes emotions that are hard to match. The banter between rival fans in the football stands is all part of the football experience too. From the witty chants that echo around the stands to the back-and-forth jibes exchanged in the pub after the match, banter is an art form in itself. It's sharp, often brutal but always good-natured, or at least it's supposed to be.

> **Fun Fact:** Did you know that the world's first football club, Sheffield FC, was founded in England in 1857? It still exists today, playing in the lower leagues, a testament to the enduring love of the game.

Cricket: The Gentlemen's Game

While we are proud of our soccer stars, we know the fans' obsession can get a bit out of hand when fuelled with a few too many pints. Cricket, on the other hand, embodies the more reflective, measured side of British life. Often hailed as a gentleman's game, cricket is as quintessentially British as afternoon tea, with its roots deep in the traditions of sleepy village greens and grand stadiums alike. The pace is slower, the atmosphere more contemplative, and the matches can stretch over days – a stark contrast to the high-octane, 90-minute fever of a football match.

Cricket is a game of patience, strategy, and, some might say, endurance. Test matches can last up to five days and still end in a draw. But don't let that fool you into thinking cricket is boring. It's a game of subtlety and skill, where a single run can change the course of the match.

Cricket is as much about the atmosphere as it is about the action. It's a sport where tradition reigns supreme, where tea breaks are as important as the runs scored. The rules might seem bewildering at first (overs, wickets, LBWs) but once you've grasped the basics, you'll find the game has a rhythm that's almost meditative.

The sound of leather on willow is music to the ears of cricket fans. There's nothing quite like the sight of a batsman elegantly driving the ball through the covers for four runs, celebrated with a polite applause for a good play.

Every two years England and Australia compete in the legendary test cricket series 'The Ashes' – a test of nerves, skill and endurance that's followed with an intensity that rivals any football match, as the two nations vye for bragging rights, and a tiny urn that supposedly contains the ashes of English cricket.

The term 'The Ashes' is symbolic of good old sarcastic wit among British sports fans. It originated in a satirical obituary published in The Sporting Times newspaper, after Australia won the 1882 match at The Oval for the first time, on English soil, no less. The obituary stated that English cricket had died, and that "the body will be cremated and the ashes taken to Australia".

Like football, British cricket has been graced by legends leaving indelible marks on the game and getting knighthoods for their efforts. Sir Ian Botham, with his charismatic personality and all-round brilliance, dominated the game in the 1980s, famously turning the tide in the 1981 Ashes series dubbed "Botham's Ashes". More recently, players such as Alastair Cook (England's highest Test run-scorer) and Ben Stokes (hero of the 2019 World Cup and Ashes series) have carried the torch to inspire new generations with their skill and determination.

Cricket has also been a platform for progress and inclusivity. The rise of women's cricket has been a significant development, with the England Women's team achieving tremendous success, including winning the 2017 Women's Cricket World Cup in front of a packed Lord's crowd. Players including Heather Knight and Anya Shrubsole have become role models, showcasing the sport's expanding reach and universal appeal.

Fun Fact: The longest cricket match in history lasted for 12 days. It was played between England and South Africa in 1939 and it ended in a draw because the English team had to catch their boat home.

Rugby: Blood, Sweat and Glory

Rugby commands a passionate following in Britain, especially in Wales, where it's practically a national obsession. Unlike the theatrics of football players crying foul at the slightest tap or shirt pull, rugby is a brutal game of raw power and physicality. The players are built like tanks, and the collisions on the pitch can be bone-crunching. Shoulder pads and helmets are unheard of. That would be far too girlie. Quite unBritish. Yet despite the violence of a rugby match, in which teeth will be lost and noses broken, rugby is, at its heart, a gentleman's game of respect. The players address the referee as 'Sir' and shake hands with their opponents at the end of the match.

When the clock was ticking down to the final moments of the Rugby World Cup final with England facing off against Australia in 2003, the scores were level when Jonny Wilkinson stepped up to the mark. With nerves of steel, he dropped a goal to secure England's first-ever Rugby World Cup win. The image of Jonny's winning kick is burned into the memory of every rugby fan. It's a moment that still sends shivers down the spine of anyone who witnessed it.

In the Six Nations Championship, England, Scotland, Wales, Ireland, France and Italy battle it out for rugby supremacy. The rivalry, the passion, the sheer physicality of it all is a spectacle that brings out the best (and sometimes the worst) in the players and fans alike. Whether it's Wales' fiery anthem 'Hen Wlad Fy Nhadau' ringing out in Cardiff or the roar of the crowd at Twickenham, the Six Nations is a celebration of everything that makes rugby great.

Tennis: Strawberries and Cream Centre Court

Let's take a breather from the bruising tackles and switch to something a bit more refined... Tennis. When we talk about tennis in Britain, we're really talking about one thing: Wimbledon. Every summer, the All England Club transforms into the centre of the tennis universe, where the world's best players compete for the coveted Wimbledon title.

Wimbledon is where legends are born, such as Fred Perry, who won three consecutive titles in the 1930s, and Andy Murray, the first British man to win Wimbledon in 77 years. His victory in 2013 wasn't just a win for Andy; it was a win for an entire nation that had been waiting, hoping, and praying for that moment.

Like cricket's test matches, Wimbledon is about tradition as much as it is about competition. The all-white dress code, the strawberries and cream served to spectators and the polite applause from the crowd is all part of what makes Wimbledon so special.

Even if you're not a tennis fan, there's something magical about the summer sights and sounds of Wimbledon.
The atmosphere is respectful, almost reverential, with the occasional ripple of applause or a well-timed "Come on, Tim!" from the crowd (even if Tim Henman has long since retired).

So the next time you're on British soil, be sure to catch a match, any match. Find a spot in a pub or on a stadium seat, grab a pint, and feel the energy that pulses through the crowd. And when the ref makes a call during the football game that seems a bit dodgy, don't be afraid to join in with a hearty, "Sort it out, ref!". You'll fit right in.

Chapter 10

"Tuck In, Mate!"

Blimey! Who Said British Grub Was Boring?

> **"The British Empire was created as a by-product of generations of desperate Englishmen roaming the world in search of a decent meal."**
> — Bill Marsano

Tell me, why is British food always getting a bad rap?

British food is anything but bland or boring. We didn't bring sweet things and spices to British tables from all over the world for nothing, you know? Our cuisine is a culinary adventure through history, brimming with character and spiced with a dash of eccentricity. Every corner of the landscape reveals a new flavour, where the weather often influences what's on your plate, and where every meal is a chapter in a story spanning centuries.

Discard any preconceived notions that British food is unadventurous. Instead envision yourself wandering through a lively street market, where the hum of traders is only matched by the mouthwatering smells of freshly baked pies and sizzling sausages. Or picture a pub by the sea, where the fish is fresh, the chips are crisp, and the stories shared over a pint are as satisfying as the meal itself.

But British food is much more than the fusion of flavours from around the world. It's about how and where it's enjoyed. For every occasion there's a food to go with it; like cucumber sandwiches at cricket matches, strawberries and cream at Wimbledon and jellied eels at the seaside.

Are you ready to discover the true taste of Britain?

Let's set off on a culinary journey that's as surprising as it is delicious, where every dish offers a unique taste of the British Isles' rich and varied heritage.

From Ye Olde Feasts to the Great British Bake Off

Let's rewind the clock to the days of yore to legendary medieval feasts, when long wooden tables groaned under the weight of roasted meats, freshly baked bread and enough ale to fill a moat. This was the beginning of British cuisine, shaped by the Norman Conquest and flavoured by the far-reaching tendrils of the spice trade. Yes, that's right, long before 'bland' became an unfair label, the Brits were all about experiencing those exotic flavours.

British food began getting a bit more interesting in the Bronze age, when spices from Asia and Europe made their way to the British Isles along the Silk Road, stretching from Rome to the far east, across Egypt, North Africa, Persia, India, China and Java. Then in the 1800s the East India Company, backed by the British military, conquered the Dutch to take control of the Spice Islands in Indonesia, bringing delicacies such as nutmeg, mace and cloves to British shores.

Fast forward a few centuries to the Victorian era and you'll find that British food was on the brink of a revolution, in tandem with the Industrial Revolution, which ultimately gave rise to our institutionalised tea-drinking culture.

But perhaps the most significant turning point for British cuisine came after World War II, when the country opened its doors and its kitchens to flavours from around the world. Immigrants from India, the Caribbean, and Asia brought with them spices, cooking techniques and exotic dishes that have since become as British as, well, the Queen herself (God rest her soul).

Fun Fact: Did you know that 'chicken tikka masala' isn't actually an Indian dish?It's said to be a curry invented in the United Kingdom in the 1970s by Indian chefs trying to adapt their traditional dishes to the less spice-tolerant Western paletes.

The Full English - A Great British Breakfast

Let's start the day with the quintessential Full English Breakfast, often referred to simply as a "fry-up". This isn't your average morning meal. It's a plate piled high and armed with enough calories to fuel a small army with a complement of fried eggs, sausages, bacon, baked beans, grilled tomatoes, mushrooms and, if you're into it, slices of black pudding (blood sausage). Plus of course the toast, often slathered with butter or margarine.

The Full English is a declaration of intent to tackle the day head-on that transcends social classes, and is perfectly acceptable to have any time of day or night. Whether you're in a greasy spoon roadside café or a country B&B, the fry-up remains a great equaliser, served with pride and usually accompanied by a cup of strong tea (builder's brew).

The British Love Affair with Tea

Speaking of tea, did you know that the United Kingdom ranks third in the world for tea consumption? We actually drink more than all the tea drinkers in China with the average Brit downing up ten cups a day.

Tea drinking is an institution, a cultural cornerstone. The phrase "fancy a cuppa?" is an invitation into the very heart of British hospitality. From the ritual of afternoon tea, complete with scones, clotted cream and jam to the more everyday occurrence of a quick “brew”, tea is ever-present. Even in moments of crisis you’ll often hear, “I’ll put the kettle on”, as if a cup of tea has the power to solve all the world’s problems. In Britain, it probably does.

Check out 'Fancy A Cuppa? British Slang 101', the first book in our series for more hilarious British slang, and plenty of tea-related phrases!

SCAN ME

In Victorian times, tea drinking was a privileged passtime reserved for the elite but like the full English breakfast, tea now transcends all classes. However, the way it's prepared, served and drunk is an instant indicator of your upbringing. Throwing a tea bag in a mug for a quick cuppa and hugging it for warmth is perfectly fine in the privacy of your own home but if you find yourself at a proper tea party with bone china cups and saucers, you'll really have to mind your manners and watch where you point your pinkie.

Debunking the Myths About British Food

Let's start with the biggest myth of them all, that 'British food is bland'. Now, I'm not sure where this rumour started but it's about as true as the idea that we all walk around with umbrellas permanently glued to our hands. From the fragrant spices in a proper curry to the rich gravy that tops a Sunday roast, British food is anything but bland. If you've ever tasted a well-seasoned roast potato, you'll know exactly what I mean.

You've surely heard that the Brits love their puddings and pies. Today puddings are usually sweet desserts but in the past British puddings were meat-based. They were basically similar to pies but without the crust of pastry. Yes, they're iconic of British the average British diet but they're certainly not the be-all and end-all of British cuisine. From hearty steak and ale pies to the delicate sweetness of a summer pudding, these dishes are varied and full of flavour. So the next time someone tells you British food is just "pies and puddings", you can confidently tell them they're only scratching the surface.

Regional Specialties From Land's End to John O'Groats

Ah, regional specialties are where British cuisine truly shines; often bizarre but never bland. Let's start up north in the Scottish Highlands – home of the haggis. In the native tongue of Scottish Gaelic, haggis is called 'taigeis'. It's a savoury pudding of minced sheep offal mixed with oatmeal, suet and spices stuffed in a sheep's stomach, often served with "neeps and tatties" (that's turnips and potatoes for the uninitiated). Now, before you wrinkle your nose, let me tell you that haggis is actually delicious. And if stuffed sheep's stomach isn't your thing, there's always Scotch broth; a hearty, warming soup that's perfect for those chilly Highland evenings.

Heading down to Northern England, we find ourselves in the land of the Yorkshire pudding. This isn't just a side dish. It's a national treasure. Whether it's served as part of a Sunday roast or filled with sausages in a classic toad in the hole, the Yorkshire pudding is a versatile wonder.

And from the sheep inhabiting the valleys of the Pennines in North Yorkshire comes one of the most sought after cheeses in the British Isles... Wensleydale, to be precise. Crumbly, tangy, and perfect with a slice of fruitcake.

Fun Fact: Did you know that the UK makes about 700 different cheeses? Before World War II, there were said to be more than 3,500 local cheesemakers. After the war there were only a hundred or so. Caerphilly, Stilton, Double Gloucester and Somerset Brie are among the delectable selection of cheeses to be found around the British Isles.

Cornwall, with its stunning coastline, is the birthplace of the Cornish pasty. The coal miners' wives of Cornwall would make these hand-held parcels of pastry filled with meat and vegetables as a portable packed lunch for the miners to chew on down the pit. Today pasties are enjoyed by everyone from surfers to city slickers grabbing a midday snack. And of course, we can't talk about Cornwall without mentioning clotted cream. Slathered on a scone with a dollop of jam, it's the star of any proper cream tea.

Over in Wales, the food is as hearty as the landscape. Welsh rarebit (a posh cheese on toast) is a must-try, especially when paired with a pint of local ale. Actually, if the truth be told, Welsh rarebit didn't actually originate in Wales and, contrary to popular opinion, there's no rabbit in it either. Lamb cawl though is a traditional Welsh stew which does have lamb in it. And if you're feeling adventurous, give laverbread a go. It's made from seaweed and is surprisingly tasty when mixed with oatmeal and fried.

Finally we come to London, the melting pot of British cuisine, where jellied eels were once the pauper's daily dish. The eels were netted in the River Thames to be chopped and boiled in spicy stock then chilled to form a jelly (an acquired taste, to be sure). The East End is also home to pie and mash, a staple of the district since the Victorian era. But what really makes London special is its diversity. Wander through any market and you'll find flavours from every corner of the world, all happily coexisting in this vibrant city.

Iconic Dishes Every British Food Lover Should Know

Now let's dive into the dishes that have come to define British food. First up, fish and chips. You can't walk down a British high street without catching a whiff of this national dish of crispy battered fish, golden chips, and a generous sprinkling of salt and vinegar. It's simple, satisfying, and utterly delicious.

Then there's the Sunday roast – a meal that's less about the food and more about the tradition. Families gather around the table, tucking into roast beef (or chicken, or lamb), Yorkshire puddings, roast potatoes and vegetables, all swimming in gravy. It's a ritual passed down through generations which brings people together.

Bangers and mash is another British classic, and it's as comforting as a warm blanket on a cold day. Juicy sausages, creamy mashed potatoes, and a rich onion gravy... It's no wonder this dish has stood the test of time. And speaking of comfort food, we must give cottage pie and shepherd's pie a mention. Both are hearty, meat-and-potato dishes, with one key difference: cottage pie is made with beef, while shepherd's pie uses lamb.

Toad in the hole might have a strange name but it's a firm favourite in British households. Originating from the northern midlands, toad in the hole was a pauper's dish in the 1800s that was meant to make the most of meat by enveloping sausages in batter. Served with gravy and vegetables. It's the kind of dish that's both quirky and comforting – a perfect example of British home cooking at its best.

And now onto the desserts, where British cuisine really lets its hair down. First up, Spotted Dick. Yes, yes, get the giggles out now. But once you stop snickering, you'll discover a pud with personality – a steamed delight that's dotted with currants and absolutely drenched in custard. It's the kind of dessert that makes you wonder why we ever stopped steaming everything.

Then there's treacle tart, the sticky-sweet masterpiece that's basically an edible booby trap for your teeth. You'll need a crowbar to get your jaw unstuck, but it's a small price to pay for something so gloriously gooey.

And we can't leave out Eton Mess – literally a beautiful disaster. Imagine someone tried to make a fancy dessert, tripped and fell face first in it, got up and decided, 'Eh, close enough'. The result is a chaotic pile of strawberries, meringue, and cream that somehow works. It's a mess, but it's a delicious mess, like a piece of edible modern art.

Scones, Jam and a Good Ol' Chinwag

No exploration of British cuisine would be complete without a nod to afternoon tea, or 'high tea' as it's traditionally called, with tea and cakes. Not to be confused with elevenses though, which is tea and biscuits, taken mid-morning. So 'tea' is more than just a cup of tea. It's an event involving a great deal of etiquette as you nibble and sip away over polite conversation. Cream teas are especially challenging as you precariously balance a tiny plate on your lap and a fork that keeps sliding off it while you're trying to give your undivided attention to the conversation. There's an ever-present danger that flecks of clotted cream might end up on the walls and in the carpet as they fly off your falling fork, or you smear cream and jam on your cheeks as you bite into a scone. This high tea ritual is a true test of British class if there ever was one.

Now, before you continue, there's one debate that might have you questioning your allegiance: cream first, or jam? It's a culinary standoff as old as the hills. Cornwall insists on jam first, while Devonshire swears by cream as the base layer. It's a bit like arguing over whether the toilet roll should go over or under. But let's be honest, as long as there's plenty of both, and a nice cuppa to wash it down, does it really matter?

Well, perhaps only if you're in Cornwall or Devon!

And then there are the cakes that Britain is famous for. Victoria sponge, named after Queen Victoria herself, is a light, airy cake filled with jam and cream. Battenberg cake with its checkerboard pattern is as fun to look at as it is to eat. Whether it's a simple slice of cake or a full afternoon tea spread, this tradition is one that continues to delight, both in Britain and around the world.

The Great British Mash-Up of Tradition and Trendiness

British food today is like your nan donning a pair of skinny jeans; comfortingly familiar, yet unexpectedly bold. Long gone are the days of soggy veg and mystery meat. Now it's all about fusion, flair and a sprinkle of world-class inspiration as chefs reimagine classic British dishes with a modern spin, blending time-honoured recipes with international flavours that'll make your taste buds dance a merry jig.

Street food markets are the new playground for this culinary creativity, giving rise to gourmet fish and chips with a zing of wasabi and Sunday roasts wrapped up in burritos. It's all about taking good ol' British grub and giving it a cheeky, contemporary makeover.

With sustainability trending, farm-to-table dining is becoming the norm with restaurants sourcing ingredients from local farms, ensuring that what's on your plate is fresh, flavourful and kind to the planet. It's British food with a conscience and proof that even the most traditional cuisine can evolve with the times.

Keep Calm and Carry On Eating

As we reach the end of our culinary journey, you should see by now that British food is so much more than beans on toast.

It's a cuisine that's been shaped by history, enriched by global influences and continually reinvented by modern chefs, except for jellied eels, that is. From pies to puddings, from haggis to tikka masala, British food is a celebration of tradition, innovation, and, most importantly, flavour.

So the next time someone tells you British food is all about bland pies and boiled vegetables, you can smile, nod, and hand them a slice of treacle tart. After all, nothing changes minds like a taste of the real thing.

Chapter 11

"You Call That Tradition?"

Festive Follies and Extreme Sports

"Remember, remember, the fifth of November, Gunpowder treason and plot. I see no reason why Gunpowder treason should ever be forgot."
— John Milton (1608)

If you've ever wondered whether Brits spend their weekends sipping tea and discussing the weather, you'd be right. But you'd also be wrong. Because, hidden beneath the stiff upper lip and polite queuing there exists a deep-seated love for bizarre, downright ridiculous traditions. I'm not talking about the occasional pub quiz or friendly game of cricket (which, to be fair, is also a bit baffling). No, I'm talking about the kind of traditions that make you raise an eyebrow and ask, "Wait, they actually do that?".

Yes, we do. Welcome to Britain, where chasing cheese, pulling ugly faces, and celebrating failed acts of treason are all part of the cultural package.

Remember, remember the 5th of November

Every year on November 5th we celebrate the fact that a group of plotters failed to blow up the Houses of Parliament. I know what you're thinking; wouldn't it make more sense to commemorate a successful revolution?

Well, this is Britain, where we prefer our victories small and understated.

Guy Fawkes Night is marked by setting off fireworks (because explosives are fun), lighting massive bonfires, and burning effigies of Guy Fawkes, the Catholic mastermind behind the 'Gunpowder Plot' to assassinate Protestant King James I of England during the Opening of Parliament in November 1605. You'll often hear children reciting the old rhyme, "Remember, remember, the fifth of November..." before getting distracted by toffee apples and running dangerously close to the bonfire. It's a night of organised chaos, but rest assured, Parliament's gates remain locked tight.

Fun Fact: In Lewes, Sussex, the local community takes things up a notch by burning effigies of controversial figures. Politicians, celebrities – you name it, they've probably been torched in effigy form.

Cheese Rolling: Extreme Sports, British Edition

If you think the Olympics are the pinnacle of sporting achievement, then you've clearly never witnessed Gloucestershire's Cheese Rolling Contest. On the Spring Bank Holiday, a giant 9-pound wheel of Double Gloucester cheese is hurled down the very steep Cooper's Hill followed by hundreds of people throwing themselves after it, tumbling, crashing, and somersaulting their way to glory at the bottom of the hill. The winner is the first to catch the cheese, or at least cross the finish line alive.

Broken bones are common but what's a few bruises in the name of cheese?

Fun Fact: Local authorities considered the Cooper's Hill cheese race so dangerous that officials tried to have it shut down in 2013 but in true British defiance the locals carried on with the race anyway. Nothing comes between a Brit and their cheese.

Facing off in the Gurning Championships

Now let's talk about a talent that only the British could elevate to competitive status: pulling ugly faces. Welcome to the World Gurning Championships, where competitors don a horse collar and contort their faces into the most hideous expressions possible. Gurning competitions are thought to have begun in 1297 at the Egremont Crab Fair, named after the sour-tasting crab apple. It was a final use for an old, worn out horse collar. The competitors' goal is to pull the sourest face possible while the crowd cheers you on. Competitors with no teeth are usually the winners with their ability to squish and contort their lower lips up to their noses. It's beauty in reverse, and no, I'm not kidding.

Tommy Mattinson, a gurner so legendary he's practically a national treasure, has won the championship a record 15 times. That's fifteen trophies for looking absolutely ridiculous. What a legacy.

Hogmanay: New Year's Eve, Scottish Style

When it comes to New Year's Eve, the Scots do it right. Hogmanay is a full-on, multi-day celebration filled with whisky, fire festivals, and a tradition called "first-footing". After midnight, the first person to cross your doorstep (preferably a tall, dark, and handsome stranger) is meant to bring you good luck, and a bottle of whisky. Forget New Year's resolutions. In Scotland the year starts with a drink and some fire juggling.

> **Fun Fact**: Edinburgh's Hogmanay festival is so epic that it attracts revellers from all over the world. Thousands of people waving flaming torches parade through the

streets. It's like Halloween, New Year's, and a Viking invasion all rolled into one.

Going Nuts with Conker Battles

Ah, conkers, the childhood game of champions. Every autumn Brits head to the nearest park, gather chestnuts (conkers), string them up and smash them together in a test of strength, skill, and possibly dark magic. With your conkers on the end of a knotted string about a foot long, you swing at your opponent's suspended conker. A hit gets you another swing at it. Miss and your opponent gets a go. The goal is simply to destroy your opponent's conker while yours remains intact.

It's all very serious business. In fact some take their conkers so seriously that they'll bake or soak them in vinegar to harden them – a tactic frowned upon as cheating but widely practised nonetheless. Because if you're not cheating in conkers, are you even playing?

Loud and Proud Town Crier Competitions

Town criers are a remnant of our Roman occupation, before newspapers and when most of the population was illiterate. They were the original social media feed, standing in the town square ringing a bell and booming out the day's news for all to hear. They were protected by law as spokesmen for the king, hence the phrase 'Don't shoot the messenger'. Now, it's a bit of a novelty but the tradition lives on with competitions to see who can shout the loudest and most eloquently while dressed in 18th-century garb. You haven't lived until you've heard a town crier belt out "Oyez, Oyez!" at 114 decibels.

Maypole Dancing

Maypole dancing is the ultimate test of coordination and teamwork.The midsummer folk dance is held on the 1st of May (Pentecost) to symbolise fertility and renewal. The dancers weave colourful ribbons around a tall pole decorated with flowers while dancing in circles. The pole is a phallic or masculine symbol while the ribbons and flowers symbolise the feminine. It's a picturesque, joyous tradition that usually ends in an enormous tangle of knots. But hey, it's all in good fun, and if you end up tied to a stranger, at least you'll have something to laugh about over tea later.

Keeping the Crown Jewels Safe

Finally, we have the 'Ceremony of the Keys', a 700-year-old tradition, where every night, without fail, the Yeoman Warders (Beefeaters) lock up the Tower of London. It's all very formal with guards, lanterns, and an air of gravitas, because heaven forbid someone forgets to lock the front door of the fortress holding Britain's crown jewels.

Fun Fact: The only time the ceremony of keys was delayed in its long history was during World War II, when a bombing raid hit the Tower. But in true British fashion, they still locked up the place, just five minutes late.

When in Britain, Join the Madness

So there you have it, a whistle-stop tour through some of Britain's most bizarre and beloved traditions. Whether you're chasing cheese, setting off fireworks or pulling the ugliest face possible, you'll find that these peculiar customs are just as much about community and joy as they are about sheer ridiculousness. And who knows? Maybe one day you'll find yourself gurning in a horse collar or rolling down a hill after some cheese. If so, welcome to the club!

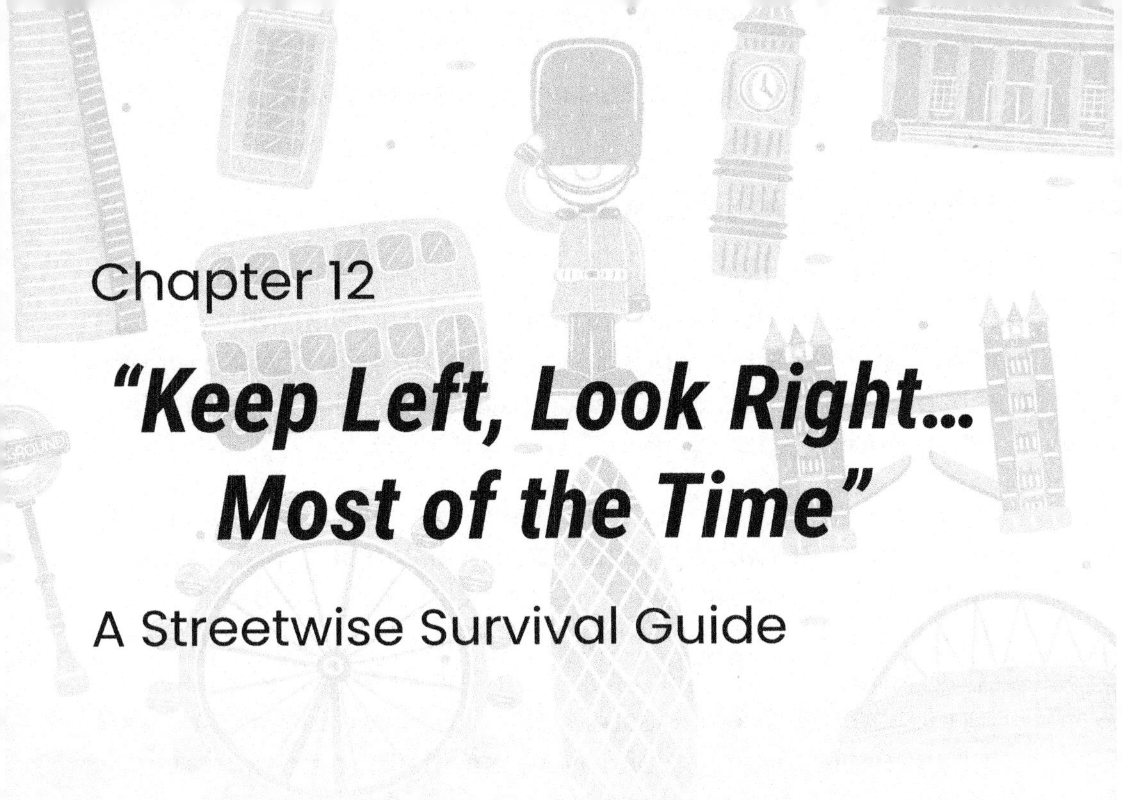

Chapter 12

"Keep Left, Look Right... Most of the Time"

A Streetwise Survival Guide

> **"I don't like being told which lane to use any more than you do."**
> — Jeremy Clarkson

Let's start with the big question, why do Brits drive on the left?

It dates back to the days of chivalry, when knights galloped around on horseback. Back in medieval times, it was essential to keep your lance arm free for a good old-fashioned joust. As most people are right-handed, knights would charge at each other on their left side of the list field. Fast forward to the 18th century and Britain decided to make this habit official by declaring left-side driving the law. So driving on the left isn't just a quirk, it's historical defiance – a reminder that the British will do things their own way, thank you very much.

Surviving Roundabouts

Learning to navigate roundabouts without stopping is a rite of passage for the urban explorer. Without a traffic light or stop sign in sight, roundabouts must be approached with a mix of caution and confidence to avoid being trapped in a never ending spin cycle.

To escape roundabouts unscathed, plan your approach like a cheetah stalking gazelles so you can slot into a gap in the herd of circling vehicles and glide out the other end without ruffling any feathers. The ultimate test in roundabout survival is navigating one of England's 'magic roundabouts'. These clusters of up to seven interconnected mini roundabouts can be found lurking in the suburban sprawls of Hemel Hempstead and Swindon, where divers have gone missing for days after their satnavs overloaded and failed. Only those sensible enough to have taken a supply of tea and biscuits have survived such ordeals. If you can escape the clutches of these seven-circle beasts, you can consider yourself a true British road warrior.

Stifling Road Rage

The motorway is another piece of treacherous terrain where subdued displays of etiquette are required to avoid alarming the natives. You'll quickly notice that merging lanes in Britain is an art of good-mannered diplomacy acted out with subtle nods and smooth manoeuvring. You're expected to glide into a lane with the calm precision of a ballroom dancer, silently thanking the other driver for their generous non-verbal invitation. Don't risk honking the horn, even if you are well versed in the happy 'thank-you' toot. Your well meaning intentions could be seen as a threat in this territory where sign-language-only rules apply.

Look Out for the Zebra Crossing!

Zebra crossings are one part of British culture that the empire didn't steal from another nation. The idea to paint black and white stripes across the road so pedestrians could cross safely is a source of national pride, and like roundabouts and lane changes, the act of crossing the road is a complex dance of etiquette.

Also called pelican or puffin crossings, depending on the crosswalk setup, the very first zebra crossing was painted across the High Street in Slough in 1951. A thousand more were trialled with great success and so it was written into the law (Highway Code) that pedestrians using them have the right of way and road users must stop to give way.

And believe me, we take this very seriously. Unlike in many other countries, drivers in the UK will automatically stop for you, even if you haven't yet set foot on the road. This often creates amusing scenarios when Brits travel abroad, where they find themselves standing indefinitely on the pavement, waiting in vain for cars to yield; a stark reminder that they aren't in Old Blighty anymore.

But there's an unwritten rule. When you do cross the road, you're expected to acknowledge the law-abiding drivers who stop for you, not with words but instead with a subtle wave or a nod conveying a silent "Thank you for not flattening me". In response, the driver often returns the gesture with a slight wave, as if to say "No problem, mate".

Keep Right and Your Eyes Down on the Tube

So you've just got your head around the idea of driving on the left. Now let's head down the long stairs and escalators to the depths of the London Underground, far below the hustle and bustle of the streets above, to the narrow train tunnels that Churchill and hundreds of Brits sheltered in during the Blitz. As we stare down into the infinite void, watching the musical billboards march by our eye level – The Lion King again and again – we are reminded once more to stand in the right place. On the left?

No! Down here the rules are different. We stand on the right, unless you're in a sharp suit, rushing to work with only seconds to spare in your rat race existence. If not then get to the right, and let the suits pass.

Affectionately known as the 'Tube', this is an underworld of unspoken rules and silent suffering, where the rules of left and right usually applied to pedestrians and traffic are flipped on their head. Every escalator has a sign saying 'Stand on the right', because nothing infuriates a Londoner more than having to walk around someone standing on the left. So if you want to blend in with the natives, stand still on the right, march up the left. And never, ever talk to anyone. This isn't social hour, you know?

Fun Fact: The "mind the gap" announcement was first broadcast on the Northern Line in 1968 and then used in all stations. The phrase was originally recorded by debonair actor Oswald Laurence, who starred in 'The Saint' and 'Sierra Nine'. His voice was replaced after he passed away in 2007, except at Embankment Station so his widow, who frequently visited the station, could still hear his voice.

The underground is a battlefield of personal space in which orbits of apologies are reduced to mere inches. When crammed together like sardines in the Tube, stick to the two-second rule to avoid the risk of catching anyone's eye. Here, where making eye contact is practically a social faux pas, staring at another passenger for more than two seconds is a high stakes game.

Silence is golden, and the loudest noise you'll hear, apart from the screech and clanking of steel wheels on decrepit Victorian tracks, is the swoosh of a newspaper being dramatically opened to signal a fellow passenger's disdain.

Up for a game of Frogger on a bike?

From the depths of the dingy underground you emerge into the slightly fresher air of the clogged city streets, where lycra-clad cyclists run the gauntlet with DoorDash delivery drivers (Dashers) and double-decker buses zooming past within inches of their handlebars. Don't be fooled by the pretty cycle lanes.They're often more like obstacle courses, shared with confused pedestrians and rogue delivery vans.

But there's a certain thrill in dodging black cabs and tourists, and once you've survived a full day of cycling in London, you'll feel like you've completed another level of the frogger - jumping from lily pad to lily pad, without getting squished. Your reward is the knowledge that you've just braved one of the world's most polite yet perilous cities.

It's a Jungle out There

Getting about in Britain means navigating a labyrinth of unspoken rules, historical quirks and polite chaos. Whether you're behind the wheel, on foot or braving the Tube, one thing remains constant: you'll need to master the British art of apologising.

If you get cut off by another car, you apologise. Accidentally nudge someone with your elbow on the bus; apologise. Glance at a pedestrian the wrong way... You know the drill – apologise. British road etiquette, like so much in this country, is dressed in a petticoat of politeness. And if all else fails, remember: keep calm, carry on, and always look the 'right' way before you cross the road.

Chapter 13

"A Penny for Your Thoughts"

Shillings, Pounds and the Euro We Never Accepted

"A fool and his money are soon parted. What I want to know is how they got together in the first place."
— Cyril Fletcher

Ah, British currency. The realm where you can carry a 'quid', a 'fiver', and a 'tenner' all in one pocket and still wonder what century you're living in. You see, money in the UK is more than just pounds and pence. It's a strange blend of history, slang, and a refusal to embrace that "foreign" Euro. So buckle up, because we're about to dive into the peculiar world of British money, where even decimalization was a reluctant revolution.

A Brief History of British Currency

Before 1971, handling British money was like solving a cryptic crossword. You had pounds, shillings, and pence. It was far from straightforward. Twelve pence made a shilling, and twenty shillings made a pound. Naturally you'd find yourself staring at a receipt wondering how 43 and ¾d could ever make sense. To this day, there are Brits who look back on those times fondly, as though juggling mathematical gymnastics in the middle of the supermarket was some sort of national pastime.

> **Fun Fact:** Did you know that Queen Elizabeth II holds the Guinness World Record for being the person whose image appears on the most currencies worldwide? She was the first British royal to have a photo featured on paper bills and her likeness is on the notes and coins of 45 different Commonwealth countries as well as the Eastern Caribbean central bank. In contrast, Queen Victoria appeared on the coinage of 21 countries while King George V appeared on 19. Talk about global domination. Britannia still clearly rules the waves.

Decimalization Day

Britain finally joined the modern world on February 15, 1971 by introducing decimalization, simplifying its currency so that 100 pence now made a pound. Sounds easy, right?

Well, the older generation still insists this was the moment the country lost its character, although everyone else was just thrilled they no longer needed a degree in advanced calculus to buy a pint of milk. The changeover wasn't smooth either. People spent months grappling with new coinage while supermarkets printed dual price labels that confused absolutely everyone. Ah, progress.

Britain's Fickle Relationship with the Euro

Despite what you might have heard, the UK was always that one partner that never fully committed to its relationship with the European Union. While the rest of Europe decided to switch to the Euro, Britain stood firmly by its trusty pound sterling. There were talks, debates, and endless newspaper articles pondering whether the UK would make the switch, but much like how they cling to tea in times of crisis, the British simply couldn't let go of the pound. After all, who would give up something as iconic as a quid?

When the UK finally broke up with the European Union in Brexit, the pound took a bit of a nosedive. Suddenly, going on holiday in Spain cost twice as much as before, and exchanging money became a high-stakes game of 'Will my currency be worth anything next week?'. But fear not, the pound is still standing, battered but unbowed. Like a stiff-upper-lipped Brit after a pub brawl, it's still hanging in there.

Modern British Money

Today British currency is a blend of tradition and technology. Contactless payments are king now. Even buskers and street performers take plastic these days, and even the most tech-resistant Brit is more likely to tap their debit card for a pint than fumble around for that rogue two-pound coin at the bottom of their pocket.

But don't let anyone fool you. Cash still reigns supreme in certain circles. Head to any rural village or buy yourself some fish and chips by the seaside, and you'll still hear someone grumble, "Sorry, cash only". It's like a rite of passage in the UK to always carry a fiver, just in case.

The Bristol Pound

And if you venture to the city of Bristol in southwest England, you might be lucky to stumble on the skeletal remains of a Bristol Pound. The now-extinct currency exclusively for Bristolians and businesses in the city had a brief existence as the first local currency to have digital and paper money from 2012 to 2021.

Keep Quirky Coins or Go Contactless?

In the UK, money is more than just a means to pay for things. It's a reflection of the country itself: quirky, traditional and not afraid to hold onto the old ways while cautiously dipping its toe into modernity. Whether you're tapping your contactless card or trying to count out change with coins that could be museum pieces, just remember: in Britain, even your money comes with a story.

Chapter 14

"I Didn't Vote for That!"

How Brexit Divided the Nation

> **"Brexit was like the UK got drunk and accidentally unfriended Europe on Facebook."**
> — Leo Kearse

Britain's exit from the European Union, "Brexit", has been called many things: a political earthquake, a national crisis, and the ultimate test of patience for the British people – like waiting for the kettle to boil only to realise you've forgotten to turn it on. But before we dive into the chaos, let's give this nation-dividing topic a little context.

Should I Stay or Should I Go?

Imagine a marriage that starts with cautious optimism, only to end in long, awkward silences at the dinner table. That's essentially Britain's relationship with the European Union after the UK joined the EU in 1973. It was never really a match made in heaven. From Margaret Thatcher's famous handbag diplomacy (banging on about "our money" in Brussels) to Tony Blair's flirtation with the euro (that never quite happened), the UK's bond with Europe was always a bit complicated, to say the least.

By 2016, the Brexit debate had reached breaking point. Immigration concerns, national sovereignty, and a growing sense of "taking back control" created the perfect storm. Then came the promise of £350 million a week for the NHS plastered on the side of a bus – a claim as enticing as it was utterly false. And so David Cameron, our ever-confident then prime minister took a gamble and put it to the vote in a referendum.

The Referendum

On June 23, 2016 Britain was divided into two camps: Leave and Remain. It was the ultimate political showdown, featuring the likes of Nigel Farage, Boris Johnson, and David Cameron. Farage, pint in hand, cheerfully waved goodbye to Europe. Boris, meanwhile, adopted his best Churchillian impersonation, promising sunlit uplands. And Cameron? Well, he placed all his chips on Remain, convinced Britain wouldn't take the plunge.

But take it the Brits did. By a slim margin of 52% to 48%, the country chose to leave the European Union. Cue the chaos. Cameron, much like a man who throws a party and then leaves before the mess, promptly resigned. "Good luck, Theresa!" he must have whispered on his way out.

Back to the Drawing Board

Enter Theresa May, Britain's new leader and the woman tasked with making sense of the senseless. "Brexit means Brexit", she declared, which was about as clear as mud. She quickly realised that figuring out what Brexit actually meant was like solving a Rubik's Cube blindfolded. Every time she tried to strike a deal with the EU, Parliament voted it down. The woman simply couldn't win. After three failed attempts, she resigned too – her tenure as prime minister defined by one word: 'Brexit'.

And then along came Boris Johnson, boisterously proclaiming he could "Get Brexit Done", storming into Number 10 Downing Street promising a swift, clean break. Spoiler alert: it was anything but. His bold threat of a No-Deal Brexit kept everyone on edge but at the last minute, like a magician pulling a rabbit from his messy mop of hair, he secured a 'deal'.... Well, sort of.

Britain officially left the EU on January 31, 2020 but the practicalities of Brexit were far from over. Trade agreements, border checks, fishing rights... The list of things to "sort out later" was about as long as the queue for the latest iPhone. But Boris, ever the optimist, declared victory and got on with the next item on his to-do list: surviving political scandal.

A Parade of Prime Ministers

As if Brexit hadn't provided enough political drama, enter Liz Truss, whose tenure as prime minister was shorter than a British summer. She promised tax cuts, growth and economic freedom but after her "mini-budget" sent the pound crashing faster than a domino line at a toddler's birthday party, she too resigned. Her stint as prime minister lasted just 49 days. Forty-nine. Even a head of lettuce outlasted her in one particularly creative British tabloid's take on the fiasco.

Finally, we arrive at Rishi Sunak, who took the helm like a weary parent cleaning up after a particularly wild house party. He was tasked with restoring stability, calming the financial markets and somehow making Brexit work. No small feat, given the political wreckage left behind.

Fun Fact: A majority of young people actually voted for the UK to remain in the EU but the divide in camps was more to do with where voters lived. Many Londoners wanted to remain, as did Scotland and Northern Ireland. However, by sheer numbers, the rest of England and Wales voted to leave.

British, European or Just Confused?

Post-Brexit Britain felt like a country with an identity crisis. Were people English, British, European or some confusing cocktail of all three?

The streets of London remained a Remainer stronghold, while towns across the North proudly flew their Leave banners. The cultural rift was glaring and causing irreparable splits between friends and families.

But true to the British penchant for brutal banter, Brexit became a goldmine for satirists, comedians, and meme-makers alike. From Boris's bumbling speeches to the revolving door of prime ministers, the absurdity of it all made for brilliant material. Political cartoonists had never been so busy. Shows like 'Have I Got News For You' dissected every twist and turn, making the British public laugh through the tears.

Brexit's Uncharted Territory

As of today, Brexit is still unfolding like a never-ending soap opera, with trade deals still being negotiated. As always, Northern Ireland remains a sticky wicket, and relations with the EU are like an awkward dance; stepping closer then drifting apart. Meanwhile, Brits carry on, heads held high, cups of tea in hand, navigating this brave new world they chose (or didn't).

So where does Britain go from here?

Like any great saga, Brexit's final chapter has yet to be written. Whether it's a tale of triumph or tragedy remains to be seen. One thing's for sure; the British, with their characteristic resilience and love of a good queue, will keep calm and carry on, even if the journey's a bit bumpier than expected.

Chapter 15

"Come Rain, Come Shine"

Gardening and the Great British Obsession with the Weather

> **"We like to talk about the weather because it's a safe topic. No one's ever lost a friendship over a debate about the rain."**
> — Peter Kay

There are only three certainties in British life: tea, queuing, and a good moan about the weather. Whether it's chucking it down or absolutely boiling, discussing the forecast is the ultimate social lubricant. Forget small talk about jobs or family. Brits are far more interested in whether you think it'll rain on Saturday. Spoiler alert: it will.

Forecast or Fortune Telling?

British weather is so unpredictable that meteorology here might as well be a branch of mysticism. Will the sunshine last more than a few minutes?

Who knows?

The odds are, the heavens will open the moment you leave the house in your shorts and you'll be soaked to the bone by lunchtime. There's a reason we don't trust the forecast. It's about as reliable as a chocolate teapot.

Furthermore, not all British weather is created equal. Scottish downpours are brutal and Cornish fog is thick enough to cut with a knife. The North and South have their own weather rivalries, too. Manchester claims the crown for having the 'most days lost to torrential rain' while Londoners grumble about their rare snow, which turns to slush in seconds.

Gardening: The True British Religion

The French have their haute cuisine and the Italians their fashion but for us Brits, gardening is our source of national pride. Whether you've got a sprawling country estate or a window box on the high street, tending to plants is as sacred as tea at four. There's something zen about mowing the lawn that taps into the British soul. If your hydrangeas aren't blooming, it might as well be national crisis territory.

Fun Fact: The quintessential English country garden with its eclectic mix of flora, fruit and veg surrounding a manicured lawn has its roots in the English Landscape Gardens that became popular at country estates in the 18th century. Until then, rather boring, highly symmetrical gardens were all the rage, because of the Normans' influence on British culture following their cross-channel invasion in the 11th century, but English architect William Kent changed all that with his idealised view of 'nature first' aesthetic, giving a proverbial two-fingered salute to the French.

The Royal Garden Party

From the perfectly manicured lawns at Buckingham Palace to the highly competitive Chelsea Flower Show, Brits elevate gardening to royal status. Winning a ribbon at Chelsea is the horticulturalist's equivalent to being awarded an Oscar, with roses and dahlias taking centre stage. If your neighbours aren't talking about the latest royal scandal, they're probably eyeing up each other's prize-winning begonias.

Likewise, the British obsession with a flawless lawn is unmatched. Striped, lush and perfectly trimmed, lawns are a source of pride and judgement. The man down the road with the perfect turf is the envy of the neighbourhood. Try using fake grass and you'll be disowned faster than a soggy cucumber sandwich at a garden party.

Allotment Armageddon

If you thought getting tickets to Glastonbury Festival was tough, wait until you try getting an allotment in Britain. These little slices of gardening heaven come with waiting lists longer than a royal coronation, and the competition to grow the juiciest tomatoes or the most enormous marrow can get fierce. The allotment wars are real.

Most Brits will wait years to get their hands on a tiny patch of soil that by the time you finally get the call, you might have grandkids old enough to inherit the plot. Still, once you're in, it's like joining an exclusive club where gossip grows as fast as the rhubarb.

The Secret Social Network

Forget Facebook. Brits prefer chatting over compost heaps and trading homegrown spuds. Allotments are the original social network, where the juiciest stories aren't just about veg but about the neighbours, too. A pint of homebrew cider shared between the bean rows can yield more gossip than a season of 'Downton Abbey'.

Rain or Shine... Mostly Rain

Gardening in Britain is less about enjoying the sunshine and more about battling the elements. Gardeners wage a constant war against the weather and don't mind a bit of mud. In fact muddy wellies are worn with pride. After all, there's no bad weather, only bad gardening attire. If the sun does show up, it's a bonus.

The British garden is a symbol of resilience, harking back again to everyday folk collectively getting through tough times during WWII. Victory gardens kept spirits (and vegetable stocks) up, and the spirit of those "dig for victory" days lives on in every modern gardener.

Come rain or shine, Brits will be out in their lots and plots, armed with a trowel, a pot of tea and an unshakable optimism. No matter how many lawns are drowned by downpours, we'll keep planting, pruning and yes, complaining, because gardening, like the weather, is unpredictable, messy and in the end, strangely satisfying.

Chapter 16

"Oh, I Do Like to Be Beside the Seaside"

Cheap Flights Abroad Vs Sandy Sandwiches

"The tearoom lady called me love. All the shop ladies called me love and most of the men called me mate. I hadn't been here twelve hours and already they loved me."
— Bill Bryson

The British seaside holiday is fast becoming a thing of the past with budget airlines offering cheap flights to sunnier destinations. Even so, the Costa del Sol just doesn't offer the same kind of nostalgic charm as a pilgrimage to Blackpool pier with a soggy sandwich in hand.

Brits have flocked to the coast for generations with an enthusiasm usually reserved for tea breaks and queueing. Come rain or shine (mostly rain), you'll be greeted by donkeys plodding across the sand and the sticky sweetness of rock candy. But behind this quaint façade lies a story of evolution, innovation, and a few questionable pastimes that can only make sense in a nation obsessed with eccentricity.

The Great Escape From Victorian Smog to Beach Huts

It all kicked off in the Victorian era when Britain's booming railways allowed holidaymakers to escape the smog of industrial towns for a breath of salty sea air. This seaside escape, with its promenades, piers and beaches dotted with daringly modest swimwear, became a signature British experience.

The great resorts of the Victorian era – Brighton, Blackpool, Bournemouth and others – became destinations of choice to escape the city. Brighton was the cool, edgy cousin, Blackpool the riotous sibling with neon lights and daring rides, and Bournemouth... Well, Bournemouth was where you went to breathe fresh air and pretend it didn't rain as much as everywhere else.

Fun Fact: Did you know that the Victorians are credited with the invention of the beach hut? They started out as 'bathing machines', which were wooden huts on four wagon wheels. The huts were moved into the water to give women privacy away from prying eyes in this age or prudeness.

Arcade Machines, Fish 'N' Chips and Pesky Seagulls

The essence of a British seaside holiday can be summed up in a few core childhood experiences: penny arcades, fish and chips, donkey rides, and the relentless battle with very determined seagulls.

You'll notice that activities such as swimming and water sports are not among the things Brits tend to do at these Victorian seaside towns. The cold, murky water is as about as inviting as a cup of cold tea. Instead we get our thrills at the penny arcades on the piers.

There's a raw thrill in feeding a 50p coin into a machine that promises riches yet delivers exactly zero reward, except the hope that the next coin will be different. Spoiler: it won't be. The prize you're angling for, a plastic keyring worth approximately 2p, eludes your grasp with a fiendish glee.

The seaside fish and chips experience is an almost spiritual moment where you wrap yourself in the aroma of deep-fried batter and thick-cut chips drowning in vinegar. It doesn't matter that you're huddled against a gale-force wind that's sand blasting your chips.This is seaside bliss... Being blissfully unaware, that is, that the seagulls have been plotting a strategic airstrike on your meal since the moment you entered the chip shop.

Docile Donkey Rides

Donkey rides, a tradition that has thankfully now been left in the past, offers a quaint glimpse into a simpler era. Picture this: a child atop a long-suffering donkey, meandering down the beach at a pace slow enough to encourage existential pondering. The donkey, looking both mildly bored and strangely resigned, seems to say, "This is my life now".

Punch and Judy Chaos: The Puppet Show That Refuses to Die

No seaside experience is complete without sitting on the seafront, watching a man beat the living daylights out of his wife, assault a policeman and wrestle a crocodile.

Children gather to watch as Mr Punch, a maniacal figure with a penchant for extreme domestic violence, clubs his way through a series of adventures, all while bellowing his signature catchphrase, "That's the way to do it!".

It's all harmless fun on the stage of a miniature Punch and Judy theatre that's been an integral part of the family entertainment on the seafront for more than 300 years.

In any other context, you'd call child services. But here at the seaside it's tradition! The audience, children and parents alike, laugh as Punch battles with crocodiles, policemen, and a host of other characters in a moral tale that's as ethically questionable as it is entertaining.

This chaotic one-man puppet show performed in a tent no bigger than a phone box has survived centuries of cultural shifts since first arriving on British shores from Italy in 1662, originally performed by the 'Comedia dell'Arte' (Comedy of Art) troupe.

The Victorian holidaymakers loved it but Punch's wife-beating antics have always been controversial with concerned parents complaining since its beginnings in Britain more than 360 years ago that the puppet violence isn't suitable for children.

In recent years, numerous seaside town councils have attempted to shut down Punch and Judy shows in sporadic fits of political correctness, only to face fierce public backlash with demands that the puppet show be immediately reinstated, at taxpayers' expense.

And so the Punch and Judy show remains a quintessential part of British seaside entertainment that we're reservedly proud of and seems set to stay for another few hundred years... It's just another example of traditional British culture that we imported and adopted as our own.

Smashing Teeth on Pieces of Rock

When you go to the seaside you're supposed to go home with pieces of souvenir rock for your friends. These are not pretty pebbles you've collected on the beach. They are colourful sticks of rock candy rolled into a sticky, tooth-destroying stick with the seaside town's name magically embedded all the way through it. It's a seaside treat that every child demands and every parent regrets buying within minutes of the first sugar-fueled tantrum. You can always spot the tourists. They're the ones diligently trying to figure out how to eat it without looking like they're auditioning for a new series of 'Survivor'.

21st-Century Seaside Staycations

With the rise in popularity of 'staycations' (holidaying closer to home), these seaside towns once on the verge of extinction are experiencing something of a renaissance with 'world-class' beach lodges and yoga retreats now on offer beside the seaside.

The old seaside favourites endure, however, because there's something comforting in the familiarity of it all. Take a stroll along the beachfront and you can still find Punch giving his wife a good seeing to and a solitary donkey plodding along the sand, resigned to its fate of forever ferrying shrieking children up and down the beach.

Chapter 17

"Flying the Flag"

The Story Behind the Iconic Union Flag and What It Represents

> **"I believe that the Union Flag should change now to reflect the four nations of the United Kingdom – England, Scotland, Northern Ireland and Wales."**
> — Ian Lucan

There's something about the Union Jack (or Union Flag, if we're being picky) that Brits just can't resist. Like a celebrity at a garden party, it's everywhere: from royal events to tea towels. Tourists slap it on anything they can carry home, while the British themselves treat it with the kind of casual respect usually reserved for an old family heirloom. It's draped at Buckingham Palace, yet you can find it on flip-flops at the local market. In short, it's not just a flag, it's a lifestyle accessory.

The Missing Welsh Cousin

The Union Flag is like the ultimate symbol of compromise. A little bit of England's St. George's Cross, a dash of Scotland's St. Andrew's Cross, and a sprinkle of Ireland's St. Patrick's Cross is stitched together in a grand design meant to scream "unity". But what about Wales?, you ask. Well, Wales is like the forgotten sibling in the family photo, perpetually out of frame. There's no red dragon or green from the Welsh flag because even though Wales is one of the countries making up the United Kingdom, it was already united with England as a principality under the British crown, almost 200 years before the union of Scotland, Ireland and England in 1801.

Fun Fact: More than 30 overseas territories around the world fly the Union Jack or have incorporated it into their own flags. Even the US state of Hawaii's flag includes the Union Jack, because the islands were once under England's protection.

Flags, Identity and the Curious Case of Context

One of the most intriguing things about the Union Flag is how its meaning changes depending on where you see it and who's waving it. It's the ultimate shapeshifter: a symbol of royal grandeur one moment, a political statement the next. Waving it on a royal birthday is patriotism. Using it in a protest march though? Well, that's a different kind of statement altogether.

Over time the Union Jack has developed a complicated relationship with nationalism, identity, and even protest. One minute it's a badge of pride, the next it's a talking point at political rallies. It's a flag that wears many hats. Sometimes it's a bowler, other times, it's more of a flat cap with an edge.

Flying the Flag: When, Where and Why it Matters

So when exactly should the Union Flag be flown?

Traditionally it's raised for royal events, sporting triumphs and of course national holidays. But these days, it's just as likely to appear on social media posts or during political protests, causing eyebrows to raise depending on the context.

It's a curious thing... The same flag that symbolises unity for some can represent exclusion for others. And while the Union Flag is a fixture at events like the Olympics, where

Britain is proudly waving its collective hand in the air, it has also become the centrepiece of intense discussions about identity. When the Union Jack appears at a march or a rally, it sometimes seems to ask more questions than it answers.

The Flag in a Post-Brexit Britain: A Midlife Crisis?

And here we are, post-Brexit, where the Union Flag finds itself in a bit of a bind. Once the flag of an island nation playing in the global leagues, it now flutters listlessly in a world where Britain's relationship with the EU has dramatically changed. You can almost imagine the flag having a bit of a midlife crisis, wondering, "Do I still represent unity or has this breakup changed me?".

Brexit may have left the Britons questioning their place on the world stage but one thing's for sure; the Union Flag is still flying, even if it's now pondering what it means to be British in this new era. It's the flag equivalent of staring into the fridge at 2am, thinking "What now?".

Long May It Wave (Even if It's a Bit Confused)

Despite its complex history and evolving symbolism, the Union Flag remains a key part of British life; sometimes proudly, sometimes controversially. Whether it's hanging over royal palaces or used as a tea towel at your local charity shop, the flag endures. Like Britain itself, it's a bit complicated, a little unpredictable, but always up for the occasion.

So the next time you see the Union Flag waving in the breeze, take a moment to appreciate all the history, pride, and occasional confusion stitched into its stripes. It's more than just a flag. It's a snapshot of a nation in all its gloriously quirky and sometimes conflicted glory.

Chapter 18

"Lovely Jubbly!"

The British Invasion of TV Sitcoms, The Beatles, Bowie and Beyond

"This time next year, we'll be millionaires!"
— Del Boy

It all started with the swinging sixties. No, not your nan's groovy living room, but the explosion of British music onto the global stage. The Beatles, those four mop-topped lads from Liverpool, conquered the world with charm. With hit songs Love Me Do and Let It Be, The Beatles rewrote what it meant to be global superstars. Following closely behind were the Rolling Stones, who were happy to be the bad boys while The Beatles wore their charm on their sleeves. Throw in a dash of The Who smashing guitars and the anti-establishment Sex Pistols pushing for anarchy and you've got the British Invasion with Johnny Rotten as the voice of punk, and Sid Vicious as the attitude.

The 70s brought us glam rock in full-blown Technicolor and took pop music to new heights with David Bowie's androgynous alter ego Ziggy Stardust performing Starman on 'Top of The Pops', and Queen's Freddie Mercury strutting about in excruciatingly tight leotards.

The last remnants of rock and roll finally gave way to the Britpop boom In the 90s. The only thing memorable about that era was the rivalry between Oasis and Blur, and Wonderwall becoming the anthem for anyone with a guitar (and even some who shouldn't have one). Meanwhile, Adele has been making sure the world knows exactly how we feel about heartbreak ever since.

The Glastonbury Effect: Festivals, Gigs and Mud

When it comes to live music, the UK doesn't just show up, it sets the stage. Glastonbury is more than just a festival; it's a rite of passage – a pilgrimage through rain and mud to see legendary live performances. Whether it's Beyoncé bringing the house down, Radiohead making everyone question their life choices, or the Arctic Monkeys proving the north has some serious musical chops, Glasto has it all.

Meanwhile, smaller festivals across the country such as Reading and Leeds keep the indie spirit alive. But one of the most anticipated annual festivals in London is the Notting Hill Carnival – a celebration of Caribbean culture, music and just about everything in between, held every year over the August Bank Holiday weekend.

TV Treasures: Monty Python, Downton, and Dodgy Dealings in Peckham

Dominating the world's pop music scene wasn't enough though. The Brits also took over the small screen with comedy classics and period dramas that have been exported all over the world and even shaped our language and mannerisms. 'Monty Python's Flying Circus' introduced the world to a new breed of quintessentially British sketch comedy. The Pythons invented surrealism with dead parrots, killer rabbits and the hysterical ministry of silly walks.

An entire generation grew up on a TV diet of the comedic genius of shows including 'The Young Ones', 'Blackadder' and

'Only Fools and Horses', which aired for a whopping 22 years as the nation waited with bated breath in their living rooms to see if Del Boy, the dodgy dealer from Peckham and his brother Rodney, would ever strike it rich. Del Boy's "this time next year we'll be millionaires" mantra had everyone rooting for these two lovable, dodgy-dealing underdogs. "Lovely jubbly" indeed.

Skip ahead a few decades to the deadpan comedy Brits are best at, 'The Office' (the original, of course, not American version), which brought the awkwardness of everyday British office life to a global audience. Who would have thought a Slough-based paper company could make millions laugh (and cringe)?

Then suddenly British drama became as prestigious as the Queen herself with 'Downton Abbey', which wasn't just a show about posh people doing posh things. It was an international sensation and an insight into the bizarre plot twists in the lives of the British aristocracy and their servants.

Meanwhile 'Doctor Who' and his time-travelling Tardis were popping onto screens in the longest-running sci-fi show, airing for 26 years from 1963 to 1989, then resuming in 2005. You're welcome, world.

Exporting Dry Wit and the Absurd

British humour, with its sharp wit and dry delivery, has been baffling and delighting audiences worldwide for decades. Shows like 'Fawlty Towers' turned everyday disasters into comedic gold, and when Ricky Gervais steps up to the podium to present the Golden Globes awards, his British banter and edgy sarcasm has the world collectively cringing and laughing.

Britain on the Big Screen

When it comes to cinema, British film makers aren't as prolific as their Hollywood counterparts but they have delivered two of the most iconic and successful film franchises ever. British writer Ian Flemming's James Bond burst onto the silver screen in 1962 in Dr. No. Since then the UK-based 007 franchise has produced more than 25 films featuring the MI6 secret service agent with a licence to kill, making it among the world's top five highest-grossing film franchises, surpassed only by the fantastical adventures of the wizard residing in The Cupboard under the Stairs at 4 Privet Drive, Harry Potter. The films, based on seven books written by J.K.Rowling about 'the boy who lived' have made Warner Bros a lot of money and the fictitious Hogwarts School of Witchcraft and Wizardry has become an empire in the real world as the set for the highest-grossing motion picture series in history.

Fun Fact: Harry Potter's childhood home, 4 Privet Drive, Little Whinging, Surrey is actually located at 12 Picket Post Close in Bracknell, Berkshire, about 40 miles west of London. The house was put on the market in 2016 for any 'muggle' to buy for the princely sum of £475,000 ($620,000).

Making Light of the Dark Side of Life

There's much more to British cinema than wizards and martinis though. Quirky comedies are a speciality of the British film industry, often forcing us to face the dark side of society and taboo topics with gritty realism and twists of dark humour. The 1996 British black comedy-drama Trainspotting directed by Danny Boyle and starring Ewan

McGregor showcased the grit and grime of the UK, while The Full Monty made male stripping oddly heartwarming. The romantic comedy set in sunny Somerset, Four Weddings and a Funeral, became the highest-grossing British film in history at the time. The British Film Institute ranked it as one of the 100 greatest British films of the 20th century, solidifying Hugh Grant's status as the stammering, charming everyman of rom-coms everywhere.

Books, Poetry and Quirky Britishness

The bounty of British literature, from the sonnets of Shakespeare to the novels of Jane Austin, has been exported around the world for centuries. Charles Dickens had readers empathising with orphans while Agatha Christie made sure no one trusted anyone at dinner parties ever again. Sherlock Holmes, the world's most famous fictional detective, has been reimagined so many times that he's basically immortal, much like Doctor Who.

The word 'orwellian' is now part of our vocabulary to describe anything resembling George Orwell's ominous vision of a dystopian society in 1984; a cheery little tale of Big Brother always watching you in a world devoid of individuality. Just take a journey on the London Underground to see this orwellian nightmare in the real world.

Away from the daily grind, the English countryside was the backdrop for J. R. R. Tolkien's tales of The Hobbit, which proved that even short people from the Shire can go on grand adventures (with second breakfasts).

Keep Calm and Carry on Invading

From the Beatles to Bond, British culture has left an indelible mark on the world. Whether it's a tear-jerking Adele ballad, a raucous Monty Python sketch or a gripping James Bond chase scene, the UK's exports have woven themselves into the fabric of global entertainment. So next time you find yourself belting out "Bohemian Rhapsody" or quoting Basil Fawlty, remember: the Brits gave us all that, and a bit of dry weather chat on the side.

Chapter 19

"Now, Don't Get Me Wrong"

Understanding the Nuances of British Conversation

> **British humour is very cruel. It's my favourite kind of humour; if it isn't cruel and funny it doesn't really cut the cake for me.**
> — Jason Sellards

British conversation is an art form in itself, where what's said is often far less important than what's left unsaid. If you're expecting directness, you might want to sit down, pour yourself a cup of tea and take a breath. British conversation is a delicate dance of politeness, subtext, and enough sarcasm to flood a very dry desert. In this chapter, we'll guide you through the maze of verbal subtleties, where understatement reigns supreme and agreeing with someone might just mean you disagree entirely.

The Art of Subtext

In British English a simple phrase like "That's interesting" can hide a world of meaning. While it sounds like a polite expression of intrigue, in reality it often translates to "I strongly disagree" (but I'm far too polite to argue). The British are experts at concealing discomfort or disapproval behind friendly facades, letting the subtext do most of the heavy lifting. It's not what you say, it's how you say it.

A drawn-out "Oh, that's interesting" likely means they think your idea is terrible but are too reserved to say so directly. This leads us nicely into another staple of British conversation...

The Understatement

The British are world champions in the art of understating the gravity of a situation to make it sound far less dramatic than it actually is.

A complete disaster might be described as "a bit of a mess" and a monumental achievement might be shrugged off with a humble "Not bad, I suppose". This is a country where a tornado could be described as "a bit of wind" and a heart-stopping roller coaster ride as "quite a lark". The less you play something up, the better – whether it's an event, an emotion, or dropping your sandwich on the Tube.

If you're expecting any show of emotion in conversation, sorry to disappoint you. Brits have a profound allergy to emotional excess in public, meaning they will often hide their feelings behind dry wit, sarcasm or an extra biscuit.

The beauty of understatement is that it allows for conversation without the messiness of over-expressing emotion, which would be terribly un-British!

Polite Evasiveness: The "Maybe" That Means "Never"

Directness is a rare gem in British conversation. If someone says, "I'll have a think about it", don't hold your breath waiting for a follow-up. This phrase, along with others such as "I'll get back to you" or "We'll see", is the British way of rejecting your idea while giving you just enough hope to think it's still on the table. It's like we never say 'never', even if we really mean 'never'.

A question like "Are you free this weekend?" might be met with, "I might be. Let me check", which translates as, they certainly aren't free but they don't want to hurt your feelings by saying so.

Sarcasm With Surgical Precision

If politeness is the shield, sarcasm is the sword. And no one wields it better than the British. Sarcasm is delivered with such deadpan precision that you may find yourself wondering if the person is serious or just being exceptionally witty.

Take this classic exchange during a torrential downpour:

"Lovely weather for the time of year, isn't it?""Yes, perfect beach day!"

Sarcasm is the unofficial language of British friendship. If someone says "oh that's so clever of you", there's a solid chance they don't mean it as a compliment. But don't worry, it's all part of the charm, probably.

Tone is Everything: The Many Shades of "Yeah, Right"

The same words can mean vastly different things depending on the tone. Take the phrase "Yeah, right". If said with a straight face, it might mean agreement. But draw it out with a hint of scepticism, and it's sarcasm in full force, meaning "I don't believe you for a second". The British have mastered the subtle art of tone-shifting to communicate everything from enthusiasm to utter disbelief.

From Bollocks to Blimey! The British Slang You Never Learned in School

One minute you're "knackered" (exhausted), the next you're "chuffed" (delighted), and when things go wrong, they're just "pants" (terrible). If you've already devoured Fancy a Cuppa? British Slang 101, you're miles ahead. If not, what are you playing at? It's your essential guide to talking like a true Brit (Shameless plug? Definitely. Worth it? Absolutely).

Scan the QR code and get started.

SCAN ME

Keep It Light, Keep It Polite

In the end, participating in British conversation is all about listening to what's left unsaid, interpreting the subtext and embracing the delicate balance of sarcasm and understatement. It's a game of wit where politeness can mask all sorts of meanings.

Mastering British chit chat is like mastering cricket; it's complicated, full of confusing rules and best enjoyed with a cup of tea. The British are masters of talking without really saying anything. So when in doubt, keep your tone polite, your sarcasm sharp and your directness safely tucked away.

Oh, and if you get lost in a conversation, just throw in a "cheers" and you'll be fine.

If all else fails, remember to smile and say "sorry". You can always change the subject to the weather or offer to put the kettle on. Either way, you'll fit right in.

Fun Fact: Although the British have a penchant for saying sorry for the tiniest of inconveniences, or even when it's not our fault, we just can't seem to find the right words when it comes to owning up to the really bad decisions we make. Instead, cue British songwriting legend John Lennon, whose song Jealous Guy is ranked by Billboard as the No. 1 apology song of all time.

Chapter 20

"Altogether Now: Let's clap for the NHS"

How the UK Handled COVID-19

> **"Anyone who works in the NHS has superpowers. It's a miracle, it is magic."**
> — Benedict Cumberbatch

The UK's approach to handling COVID-19 could be summed up as a stiff upper lip, a bit of confusion, a lot of queuing and bizarrely, weekly rounds of clapping. This chapter dives into the quirks, the chaos and the community spirit that defined Britain's experience of the pandemic, from the rise of toilet paper stockpiling to virtual pub quizzes, and how we all awkwardly came together while staying apart. Welcome to the bizarre world of pandemic Britain.

"Stay Home, Protect the NHS, Save Lives"

The government's response to the pandemic was encapsulated in the slogan 'Stay Home, Protect the NHS, Save Lives'. The public health mantra centred around supporting the National Health Service (NHS) was the subject of countless memes. It was plastered everywhere; on TV, social media, billboards and buses. It was simple, direct, and very, very British – almost as British as the complete and utter panic that ensued.

Shelves Wiped Clean by Toilet Paper Hoarders

We'll all remember The Great Loo Roll Shortage of 2020, when the British public collectively decided that the most important commodity during a respiratory virus outbreak was toilet paper, obviously. Supermarket shelves were wiped clean (pun intended) as panic buyers hoarded rolls of Andrex like they were preparing for a hundred-year siege. There was no rhyme or reason to the panic buying – just pure, unbridled fear of the unthinkable: running out of loo roll.

Meanwhile, Prime Minister Boris Johnson's initial approach involved "herd immunity", a concept that sounded suspiciously like "just let everyone get sick". However, after a few weeks of that not being the best PR move, the government swiftly pivoted to "Actually, never mind. Let's lock down".

How NHS Workers Were Paid With Claps

In a spontaneous outpouring of camaraderie, Brits began a weekly ritual of clapping for the NHS. Every Thursday at 8 pm, the citizens stepped outside, armed with enthusiasm, pots, pans, and anything that could make a decent amount of noise. It was our way of saying "thank you" to the NHS workers on the front lines. For a few brief minutes, there was unity. Neighbours you'd never spoken to (or possibly didn't know existed) were suddenly there, banging kitchenware and waving across the road.

Sure, there was some irony to it. You couldn't help but wonder if the NHS staff, who were actually risking their lives, might have preferred a pay rise over a weekly symphony of mismatched clattering. Nevertheless, the clapping continued, evolving into a form of competitive sport. Some families brought out drums while others set off fireworks. No one wanted to be out-clapped.

But after several weeks the enthusiasm began to wane and people quietly retreated back indoors, wondering how much longer they could keep this up, and whether their neighbours would notice if they skipped a week.

From Pub Banter to 'Can You Hear Me Now?'

One of the biggest casualties of lockdown life was the Great British Pub. The heart of British social life was temporarily closed and Brits everywhere mourned the loss of a cosy corner to sit and hug a beer. Getting rounds in was replaced with Zoom quizzes, where you could drink on camera while answering obscure trivia questions in a group video call. It wasn't quite the same as going down the pub for a bit of banter but we made do all the same.

The phrase "work from home" soon became synonymous with "work from bed" and productivity levels took a nosedive as the nation collectively decided that loungewear was an acceptable uniform for just about everything. Why bother with a suit and tie when you can wear pyjamas to your 9 am Zoom meeting?

Pro-tip: only switch on the camera if you've bothered to get out of bed.

Social distancing, meanwhile, played into the hands of the introverted Brit. We were finally given an official reason to avoid small talk with strangers. You want us two metres apart?

Bliss!

Those awkward encounters in the street side stepping each other were gone. A polite nod from a distance sufficed. It was everything us reserved Brits secretly dreamed of.

Fun Fact: With people working from home during lockdowns, air quality in major cities drastically improved with nitrogen dioxide (NO2) levels dropping to about half the normal amount in London, Birmingham, Bristol and Cardiff.

Embracing the "New Normal"

Locked in our homes, us Brits found solace in discovering new hobbies that rekindled the nostalgia of the good old days of hunkering down during the wars. Baking in particular became a national pastime. Banana bread was suddenly everywhere, as were attempts at DIY. Every other person was either tiling a bathroom or building a shed during the lockdowns. We were doing more gardening than ever and the queues at hardware stores like B&Q were longer than the lines for trendy nightclubs in Shoreditch.

Elbow Bump Greetings

The pandemic also killed off the handshake. Now, the once-simple act of greeting someone became an awkward dance of uncertainty. Do we nod, wave or bump elbows?

Some of us went for the 'awkward hover', where you stand there with a hesitant smile, unsure if it's safe to touch another human yet.

Ultimately the forced introversion didn't suit our neighbourly nature. Mental health took a hit and the Brits, known for their stoicism, suddenly found themselves discussing their feelings. That was new but we got through it, mostly with cups of tea and sarcasm.

Surviving on Memes, Masks and Mugs of Tea

So, what did we learn from the lockdowns?

Britain handled the pandemic with a mixture of resilience, occasional chaos and more than a few cups of tea. Whether it was clapping for the NHS, forming socially distanced queues, or baking an unnecessary amount of bread, we found a way to keep calm and carry on. Did it bring us closer together or highlight our divisions?

That's hard to say but if one thing is certain, Brits will always find a way to make light of even the darkest times. And yes, we're still waiting on that NHS pay rise but at least we've got plenty of banana bread to go around.

Chapter 21

In Conclusion

A Jolly Good Send-Off!

> **"He who laughs most, learns best."**
> — John Cleese

Well done, old chap (or chapette)! You've made it through all the politeness, the weather chat, the never-ending queues, and even survived the baffling chaos of Brexit. You've officially completed your crash course in Britishness, and what better way to celebrate than with your very own British Survival Kit? (Certificate of Britishness included, of course).

The British Survival Kit: Because You're Going to Need It

1. **A Stiff Upper Lip:** For those moments when the rain begins just after you've taken off your coat, or your train gets cancelled again, leaving you stranded in Nowhere-upon-Drizzle. Keep calm and carry on, friend.

2. **A Portable Tea Bag:** Life without tea is not a laughing

matter. Keep this on you at all times for emergencies such as long queues, tedious small talk or when your inner monologue begins to wonder whether it's too early for a cuppa. Hint: It's never too early.

3. **An Emergency Apology Note:** For bumping into doors, chairs, and occasionally your own shadow. This pre-written note will get you through all those "sorry-not-sorry" moments. You're British now; apologising is your superpower.

4. **The Sarcasm Decoder:** Essential for translating the endless nuances of British wit. Remember, "Oh, really?" can be either innocent curiosity and a devastating takedown, depending on the eyebrow angle.

5. **Queueing Shoes:** Sturdy, comfortable and durable. Whether you're in line for a bus or the post office, you'll be well-equipped to stand in line.

6. **A Flimsy Brolly**: With the ever present threat of rain when you get all four seasons in a single day, always have an umbrella at the ready for a shower or a downpour.

Your Official Certificate of Britishness: You've Earned It!

CERTIFICATE OF COMPLETION

Congratulations!

You're officially British!

Awarded to ....

Date ....

A Humorous Look Back: Your Britishness in Review

As we reflect on your journey, let's take a moment to appreciate the skills you've mastered:

- **Politeness Bootcamp:** You've learned the fine art of the British apology. Whether you meant it or not, it was heartfelt (sort of). You're now fluent in saying "sorry" when it's entirely unnecessary and not your fault.

- **Queueing Olympics:** You've earned a gold medal in waiting patiently and spotting the correct end of the queue. Never forget, the last person to join is your nemesis, but smile politely anyway.

- **Tea Mastery:** From builders' brew to Earl Grey, you've cracked the code of the perfect cuppa. Pro tip: It's always the right time for tea. Always.

- **The Royal Soap Opera:** You're now a certified expert in British monarchic drama, from 'The Crown' to tabloid headlines. And yes, you now have opinions on swan ownership.

- **Pub Banter Champion:** Whether it's ordering a pint or throwing in some cheeky remark, you've got this. Just don't forget whose round it is and remember you've got to pull your weight in the great British pub rotation.

- **Brexit Masterclass:** Still confused? Excellent! That's the mark of a true Brit. Remember, the more complicated it sounds, the better you've understood it.

You've been equipped with all the essentials to blend in and thrive in the wilds of British society. Just remember, your Certificate of Britishness comes with great responsibility. Use it wisely, and never forget the golden rule: Keep Calm and Carry On (even when the Wi-Fi cuts out).

Good luck on your continued adventure and remember, when in doubt, queue politely, sip your tea, and try not to step on any swans.

The Britishness Quiz: How British Are You, Really?

Now it's time to put your newfound Britishness to the test. Think you've got what it takes to blend in like a local?

Take the British Culture Quiz and find out whether you've truly mastered the art of Britishness. Scan the QR code, have a laugh, and see if you can out-Brit even the Brits.

Spoiler: There's no prize, but you might earn bragging rights for the next pub quiz.

Scan the QR code below to access the free quiz.

SCAN ME

One Last Favour

If this delightful romp through British culture gave you a chuckle or two (or perhaps a well-deserved eye roll), please take a moment to leave a review on Amazon. Your thoughts mean the world to us, plus it helps us keep the tea flowing and the queue moving. Simply scan the code and share your British transformation with the world.

Who knows, maybe you'll inspire someone else to embrace the joy of queuing and the fine art of tea-making?

Cheers, mate!

Printed in Great Britain
by Amazon

54588826R00086